F

An Examination of the
Nancy Cooper Murder Case

Lynne Blanchard

Book Layout © 2015 BookDesignTemplates.com

Framed / Lynne Blanchard --

ISBN 978-1537643304

CONTENTS

Preface

I was initially drawn to this fascinating case because it was local. I had never seen a trial, so when a news station streamed it live, I watched with interest . . . and over time with concern. I became very disturbed by what I was witnessing. It truly opened my eyes to the horrible state of our justice system. I ended up researching the case in depth over a span of four years. This book exposes the unfairness and official misconduct that occurred from the beginning of the investigation and throughout the legal proceedings.

This book was originally published as *Framed With Google Maps* – The Truth About the Brad Cooper Case.

{ 1 }

Nancy Disappears

The entire community was frantically searching for Nancy Cooper—wife to Brad, mother to Bella and Katie. She left for a run the morning of July 12, 2008 and never returned.

Friday, July 11, 2008

Nancy Cooper was up by 5 o'clock a.m., which was typical for her. She had plans to go running with her friend, Carey Clarke. The two of them were training together for an upcoming half-marathon, but Nancy didn't feel like running that morning, so she called Carey and cancelled. She told Carey she would speak to her soon to schedule another run.

Later that morning, Nancy took the girls—Katie, 2 and Bella, 4 to a community pool at her friend, Hannah Prichard's neighborhood. She stopped by a deli on the way to grab lunch for everyone. The girls swam and played while Nancy chatted with Hannah. She was complaining about Brad that day—how he'd forgotten to leave her cash as part of their agreed upon budget. She called Brad at work a few times to remind him that he'd forgotten, and he offered to leave work and bring her some cash, but Nancy told him it was okay, not to bother.

Mid-afternoon, Nancy took the girls and headed home to get ready for a neighborhood party that her friends, Craig and Diana Duncan were hosting. She had offered to cook ribs for the party so she stopped at the grocery store on her way home to purchase them.

As she prepared the ribs, she spoke to her twin sister, Krista on the phone. Krista lived in Canada with her husband, Jim Lister. Both Nancy and Brad were born and raised in Canada before relocating to the Raleigh area in 2001 for Brad's job as a Cisco engineer. Nancy and the girls had recently taken a trip to Hilton Head Island with her sister and her parents so they talked about how things were going since they'd last seen each other on Sunday.

Nancy also spoke on the phone to Hannah as she continued preparing for the party. She told Hannah she would speak to her the next day about possibly going to the pool again. She finished cooking then got dressed for the party. She chose a new Ella Moss sun dress, which was teal with a black flowered print and flip-flops, and then she and the girls headed across the street to the Duncans' at around 6 o'clock. Brad joined them after work, arriving at approximately 6:30 p.m.

Nancy chatted with several of the guests and mentioned that Brad had "kid duty" that weekend. He spent most of his time taking care of the girls, pushing them on the swings and feeding them dinner.

While there, Brad made plans to play tennis the following morning with Mike Hiller. They both enjoyed tennis and hadn't had the opportunity to play in some time. Since Brad had cancelled on Mike in the past due to Nancy not being home to watch the children, Mike took the added measure of also confirming Brad's availability to play tennis with Nancy. She was fine with it, so Brad and Mike agreed on a time of nine o'clock the next morning. The Coopers also made plans with the Hillers (Mike and Laura) to get together the following evening to play Sequence. They had been friends with the couple since shortly after they'd moved to North Carolina.

Brad agreed to take the girls home and put them to bed so Nancy could spend more time at the party. Several of her friends were there and she was a very social person. She walked Brad and the girls home at around eight o'clock, said good-night and then returned to the party alone. She was able to relax more with the children gone and she enjoyed some of the ribs that she'd brought, as well as some avocado salad and lemon cake. She also drank several glasses of wine and a few beers and remained at the party until approximately midnight.

When she arrived home, she looked in on Brad and the girls. He had fallen asleep in the girls' room. Brad and Nancy typically took turns sleeping with the girls. Brad saw her silhouette peek in the room and then fell back to sleep. He was awakened by Katie's crying at around 4 a.m. so he took her downstairs so she wouldn't wake Bella. He tried to calm her down but noticed they were out of milk. According to Brad, Nancy soon joined him and they took turns caring for Katie while also getting some laundry done. The Coopers were early risers – Nancy often woke up early to go running and Brad to begin working, so the fact that both of them stayed up was not unusual.

Eventually they realized that the only thing that would really soothe Katie was milk so Brad went to the Harris Teeter store shortly after 6 a.m. to purchase some. Soon after he returned, Nancy complained that they had run out of detergent, so he returned to the same store once again. While en route to the store, Nancy called and asked him to also grab some Naked green juice for their older daughter, Bella. Brad enjoyed the healthy drink and soon Bella began asking for it as well.

Brad returned home and took Katie upstairs to his home office to finish her bottle. He heard Nancy yell up and ask if he'd seen her shirt, then she quickly said, "Never mind." After that, he heard the door close as she left the house at approximately 7 a.m. *That would be the last time he would ever hear her voice.*

When Nancy hadn't returned by 9, he wondered if she possibly stopped for coffee or decided to go to the gym. Nancy was independent and would often stop for coffee; however he had plans that morning and needed her to be home to watch the girls. Brad and Mike talked by phone and regretfully cancelled their tennis plans but planned to reschedule soon.

One of Nancy's friends, Jessica Adam called at approximately 9:30a.m.and asked for Nancy. Brad told her that Nancy wasn't home. Hannah also called a short time later and Brad told her the same – Nancy wasn't home.

Brad started to get very worried when lunch time approached and Nancy still hadn't returned. He called Jessica Adam to see if she had Carey Clark's number since Nancy and Carey were training together for the upcoming half marathon. He thought she may have gone running with Carey. Jessica did not have the number, so he told her he was going to put the girls in the car and drive around to look for Nancy.

Minutes later, *Jessica placed a panicked 911 call to police* and reported Nancy missing and expressed concern that Brad may have harmed her. Her statements were very odd because Brad had never hurt Nancy. There was no history of domestic abuse within their relationship. She would state that Nancy was expected at her house that morning, but it didn't make sense because Nancy had plans to watch the children that morning while Brad played tennis.

Soon after Jessica's call, Cary Police arrived at the Cooper house. They questioned Brad and organized a canine search at his request. Friends printed "missing" flyers and coordinated search teams . . . but tragically, Nancy was found dead two days later in a new construction area. Her body was visible from the road. She was face down and wearing nothing but a sports bra, which was twisted and pulled up above her breasts.

{ 2 }

Primary People Profiles

Brad Cooper – Defendant in State of North Carolina v. Bradley Graham Cooper

Nancy Cooper – Married to Brad Cooper from 2000 to 2008

Bella Cooper – Oldest child of Brad and Nancy

Katie Cooper – Youngest child of Brad and Nancy

Garry and Donna Rentz – Parents of Nancy Cooper

Krista Lister – Twin sister of Nancy Cooper

Terry and Carol Cooper – Parents of Brad Cooper

John Pearson – Former neighbor of the Coopers who admitted to a sexual encounter with Nancy in late October 2005, 9 months before Katie was born

Kinde Rawlins –Neighbor of the Coopers. Once married to John Pearson

Brett Adam – Married to Jessica Adam, last phone call to Nancy's phone the night before she disappeared was placed from his phone

Jessica Adam – Wife of Brett Adam, friend of Nancy's, called 911 to report Nancy missing

Hannah Pritchard – Friend of Nancy's

Susan Crook – Friend of Hannah Prichard and Nancy Cooper

Carey Clark – Friend and running partner of Nancy's

Mike Hiller – Friend of the Coopers, scheduled to play tennis with Brad the morning Nancy disappeared

Clea Morwick – Friend of the Coopers, watched the Cooper children on the day that Nancy disappeared

Mike Morwick – Clea's husband, expressed romantic interest in Nancy

Craig Duncan – Neighbor of the Coopers, lived directly across the street, expressed romantic interest in Nancy

Diana Duncan – Craig's wife, close friend of Nancy's, hosted the party on July 11

Ross and Damia Tabachow – Friends of the Coopers, attended the Duncans' party on July 11

Ricardo Lopez – Friend and co-worker of Diana Duncan; spoke to Nancy the night of July 11 at the Duncans' party

Detective Adam Dismukes – Cary Police investigator

Detective George Daniels – Cary Police - lead investigator

Detective Jim Young – Cary Police investigator

Patricia Bazemore – Cary Chief of Police

Heather Metour –Nancy's best friend at one time, had brief affair with Brad Cooper 3-4 years prior, was in relationship with John Pearson at the time of the murder

Jay Ward – Defense Expert – Network Security Specialist

Giovanni Masucci – Defense Expert – Forensic Examiner

Agent Johnson – FBI agent hired by the State to analyze the computer evidence

Officer Chappell – State computer expert with the Durham Police, assigned to the FBI task force

Defense Attorneys – Howard Kurtz, Robert Trenkle

Assistant District Attorneys – Amy Fitzhugh, Boz Zellinger, Howard Cummings

Judge – Paul Gessner

Swift Creek Fire Department – Responded to location where Nancy's body was found

CCBI – City County Bureau of Identification – Assisted with crime scene evidence

{ 3 }

Brad and Nancy

Brad grew up in Medicine Hat, Alberta, Canada—a small town north of Montana. He lived with his parents, Carol and Terry Cooper, and his younger brother Grant. He had a normal and happy childhood. In the winters, he and his father would play hockey and work on projects around the house. He would often attend his dad's university chemistry classes and help out. In the summers, he would garden with his mother and grandmother, a hobby he would later enjoy with his own daughters.

Brad's family valued education and after graduating from high school, Brad attended Medicine Hat College. After one year, he enrolled in the University of Calgary to pursue a degree in Computer Science. He graduated in 1996, and began working in the computer field.

A few years later, Brad met Nancy. Once they started dating, they were inseparable. On Christmas Day 1999, Brad proposed to Nancy surrounded by her family and their love and support. They were married on October 13, 2000, in Calgary. They had originally planned their wedding for the following May, but Brad received a job offer with Cisco in the United States, and they would only give Nancy a visa if they were married. Nancy and Brad rushed the wedding before Brad accepted the job so that Nancy could obtain a visa. Nancy and Brad moved from Calgary to Cary, North Carolina on January 1, 2001. They purchased a home in the Lochmere community and began their life as a married couple.

The couple had two daughters. Bella was born in February 2004 and Katie in July 2006. Both Brad and Nancy were very hands-on with the girls. Since Nancy was a stay-at-home mom she would normally take them to preschool in the mornings, arrange for play-dates with other kids their age and take them swimming. Nancy was described as an amazing mother by friends and family.

Brad spent a lot of time with the girls when he was not working. He would often care for them evenings while Nancy was out with her friends and on weekends he took them to the museum or the pool. He especially enjoyed taking them to the Durham Museum of Life and Science which had a butterfly house and lots of activities for kids.

Brad enjoyed his job as a Cisco VoIP (Voice over Internet Protocol) engineer and decided to pursue an MBA degree at North Carolina

State University so he could advance his career. He graduated in December 2007 with Nancy, Bella and Katie by his side.

The marriage became strained in the early part of 2008 when Brad admitted to Nancy that he'd had a brief affair a few years prior. It was with Nancy's best friend at the time, Heather Metour. Heather told Nancy about the affair several months prior but Brad denied it at that time. Brad told Nancy he was sorry and that he regretted it. He wanted to remain married so they tried counseling for a few sessions, but Nancy had trust issues and decided she wanted to end the marriage.

In April 2008, Nancy had an attorney draft a separation agreement. The terms specified that the Coopers would have joint custody but that the children would live with Nancy. Nancy had planned to take the girls and move to Canada in late April 2008, but after receiving the separation draft, Brad was no longer agreeable to the move. He was unable to find a position with Cisco in Canada, and he worried he would not be able to see the children often enough, so the move was cancelled.

Over the next few months, the Coopers didn't seem to be in any great hurry to move things along with the divorce. Nancy wasn't in contact with her attorney again aside from an email or two. Brad had an initial meeting with an attorney but no one was ever assigned to work with him, and he was going to have to find a different attorney to negotiate the terms of the separation and custody.

The Coopers remained together in the same house. Brad stayed in the guest room. During this time, they continued to do many things together as a family and as a couple, such as neighborhood parties and game nights with friends. At the time of Nancy's disappearance, there were still plans to divorce but the relationship was stable.

Most people describe Brad as quiet and reserved, while Nancy was very outgoing. The Coopers had a few long term couple friends and

Nancy had a large circle of her own friends. There seemed to be a different dynamic to the longer term friendships than some of Nancy's more recent ones. This becomes important later in understanding what went wrong in this case because the newer friends actively participated in a modern day witch hunt and lines were drawn for those who did not grab a torch. Nancy had a tendency to bash Brad to her newer friends as she proceeded with the divorce plans. She didn't speak as negatively about Brad to their older friends who knew him well.

During the summer of 2008, Nancy spent a lot of time socializing with her friends— hanging out at the pool or running. She would often spend time with them in the evenings after Brad was home to watch the girls. Things were sometimes strained within the social circle and there would be on-again, off-again friendships, conflict, gossip and jealousy. There were also affairs, flirtations and betrayals.

work on projects around the house together. As long as Brad can remember, he would attend his dad's university chemistry classes and help out. In the summers, Brad would garden with his mother and grandmother, a hobby he would later enjoy with his own daughters. His family valued education. After graduating from high school, Brad went to Medicine Hat College. After one year, Brad attended the University of Calgary so that he could leave the nest. He graduated in 1996 with a degree in Computer Science. A few years later, Brad met Nancy. Once they started dating, they were inseparable. Nancy also grew up in Canada. She had an identical twin sister, Krista, a younger sister, and an older brother.

On Christmas Day 1999, Brad proposed to Nancy surrounded by her family and their love and support. They were married on October 13, 2000, in Calgary. They had originally planned their wedding for the following May, but Brad received a job offer with Cisco in the United States, and they would only give Nancy a visa if they were married. Nancy and Brad rushed the wedding before Brad accepted the job so that Nancy could obtain a visa. Nancy and Brad moved from Calgary on January 1, 2001. For the next seven years, they lived in Cary, North Carolina. Brad worked at Cisco, as a VoIP (Voice over Internet Protocol) engineer, and they had two daughters. Bella was born in February 2004 and Katie in July 2006. The next year, Brad earned his MBA from North Carolina State University. He graduated on December 18, 2007. Nancy, Bella and Katie were there by his side.

Things became strained around the beginning of 2008 when Brad admitted to Nancy that he'd had a brief affair with Heather Metour sometime around 2004. Nancy and Heather had been best friends for several years. Heather told Nancy about the affair several months prior but Brad denied it at that time. Brad told Nancy he was sorry and that he regretted it. He wanted to remain married so they tried counseling for a few sessions, but Nancy had trust issues and decided she wanted to end the marriage.

In April 2008, Nancy's parents, Garry and Donna Rentz provided her with money for an attorney to draft a separation agreement. The terms specified that the Coopers would have joint custody but that the children would live with Nancy. Nancy could take the children and move to Canada at any time. Brad would have to pay child support in the amount of $2100/month. Nancy had planned to take the girls and move to Canada in late April 2008, but after receiving the separation draft, Brad was no longer agreeable to the move. He was unable to find a position with Cisco in Canada, and he worried he would not be able to see the children often enough.

The Coopers didn't seem to be in any great hurry to move things along with the divorce. Nancy wasn't in contact with her attorney again aside from an email or two. Brad had an initial meeting with an attorney but no one was ever assigned to work with him, and he was going to have to find a different attorney to negotiate the terms of the separation and custody.

The Coopers remained together in the same house. Brad stayed in the guest room. During this time, they continued to do many things together as a family and as a couple, such as neighborhood parties and game nights with friends. At the time of Nancy's disappearance, there were still plans to divorce but the relationship was stable.

Most people describe Brad as quiet and reserved, while Nancy was always very outgoing. The Coopers had a few long term couple friends and Nancy had a large circle of her own friends. There seemed to be a different dynamic to the longer term friendships than some of Nancy's more recent ones. This becomes important later in under-standing what went wrong in this case because the newer friends actively participated in a modern day witch hunt and lines were drawn for those who did not grab a torch. Nancy had a tendency to bash Brad to her newer friends as she proceeded with the divorce plans. She didn't speak as negatively about Brad to their older friends who knew him well.

During the spring and summer of 2008, Nancy spent a lot of time socializing with her circle of friends – hanging out at the pool, exercising, lunches, evenings drinking wine and neighborhood barbecues. Things were sometimes strained within the social circle and there would be on-again, off-again friendships, conflict, gossip and jealousy. There were also affairs, flirtations and betrayals.

{ 4 }

The 911 Call

July 12, 2008

Jessica Adam placed the frantic 911 call at 1:50 the afternoon of July 12. Remember that she also expressed concern that Brad may have harmed Nancy. Her trepidation was puzzling because it occurred at a time when Nancy had only been missing a few hours. There were many possibilities for Nancy having been delayed—she may have stopped for coffee or sprained her ankle on a trail or gone to the gym to name a few. It is understandable for one to be worried about a friend's delay at returning home, but why was she hysterical?

Brad was worried too, but he responded with level-headedness as he put the kids in the car and drove around to look for Nancy. Jessica didn't even inform Brad that she'd planned to call police. Why wouldn't she have suggested that *he* call police to assist in finding Nancy?

Her baseless accusations placed Brad under immediate suspicion of police, friends, neighbors, and Nancy's family and influenced the entire investigation. Jessica would later admit that she had never even heard him so much as raise his voice to her. Nancy wasn't afraid of

Brad. Unfortunately, false accusations stick very easily and it can be next to impossible for the accused to defend against them. The Duke Lacrosse case is a good example of how quickly things can spiral out of control.

Not only did Jessica make accusations against Brad, she took an immediate active role in keeping police focused solely on him. This is an excerpt of the call to illustrate how she immediately placed suspicion on Brad.

Hi. My name is Jessica Adam and I'm calling um because a friend of mine uh has been missing since seven o'clock this morning, and um her husband and her are in the middle of a divorce and I'm not sure what the protocol would be but I . . . . she . . . she said she went out for a run this morning at 7 o'clock in Lochmere, and no one has heard from her. She was supposed to be at my house at 8, and I'm just – because of the situation with the divorce.

After that, the operator requested details about Nancy and then Jessica came straight out and accused Brad of harming Nancy.

She was expected here no later than 9 o'clock um to help me with a project and then she also had another appointment with a friend um her name is Hannah who just called me on the other line hysterical cause she's also now having the same thought that I am about her husband um if he's done something and I don't . . . I mean God forbid but (deep breath) um.

Just before ending the call, the operator told Jessica to give her some time. An officer would be dispatched to the house to talk to Brad. She instructed her to call back in an hour, but as soon as the call ended she asked her friend, Mary Anderson to drive her to the Cooper's home because she was too distraught to drive. Rather than searching the trails where Nancy would typically run, she hurried to the Cooper's home, arriving before police.

When Cary Police Officer Hayes arrived, she immediately informed him that Nancy was expected at her house to paint that morning. By the time neighbors and friends began gathering, Jessica had lost all control of her emotions and began yelling, "I know Brad *did* this!" Did what? This outburst indicates that she already knew Nancy was dead, but how was that possible . . . unless she had firsthand knowledge about why Nancy hadn't returned home.

After that, Jessica engaged in two heated arguments with friends of the Coopers. She had words with Mike Morwick when she instructed him about how to handle children during a crisis. (Mike's wife, Clea, was caring for the Cooper children while Brad talked to police.) Mike was annoyed with her and told her to stop trying to take control of the children.

Jessica had a second heated discussion with Mike Hiller. By that time she had told everyone that Nancy was expected at her house that morning to paint. Mike told Jessica that it didn't make any sense because he had plans to play tennis with Brad. Nancy confirmed that she would watch the children. She never mentioned that she had painting plans. Jessica began yelling at him and swearing "I know he 'f' ing did it!" She further told Mike not to talk to police and that she would be the point person since she was the one who called them.

Aside from accusing Brad of harming Nancy, Jessica also made other odd statements during the 911 call. She referenced that Nancy would run with Carey but then it sounded like she said "*used* to run with her." If that is indeed what she said, that indicates that she knew Nancy was dead when she placed the call. She mentioned that it was odd that Brad would call and ask for Carey's number. What is odd about that? It would have been odd if he *hadn't* called Nancy's friends to try to track her down.

Jessica also stated that it was odd that Nancy didn't tell her about any plans to run, but that didn't make sense because the two of them hadn't run together in at least a year. Nonetheless, the accusatory call steered the investigation as police did not note any red flags with the call itself or Jessica's behavior that afternoon. They accepted that her hysteria was warranted.

{ 5 }

Immediate Tunnel Vision

Brad's and Nancy's friends, Mike and Clea Morwick, cared for Bella and Katie on July 12 so that Brad could focus on providing the investigators with everything they needed to find Nancy. He showed police around the house, allowed them to take photographs, and later a canine search was organized. Brad was distraught that day, so when a friend offered to contact Nancy's parents, he gratefully accepted the offer.

Hannah Prichard and Jessica Adam helped out with childcare the next two days. When Nancy's twin sister Krista arrived in town on Sunday, July 13, she went to Hannah's house because the girls were in Hannah's care at the time. Brad later went to pick up his girls, but Krista wanted them to stay with her. He told her he needed them for the comfort, but he invited her to stay at the house. She declined.

Meanwhile, police met Nancy's parents, Garry and Donna Rentz, at the Raleigh airport and escorted them to the police station. Nancy's family as well as Brad attended a police press conference that day and thanked the community for the support in trying to find Nancy.

The next day (July 14), Brad was finally able to assist in the search for Nancy, but sadly she would be found dead later that evening.

Police tried to convince Brad to come to the station for a "proper" interview, but he declined. He preferred to stay home with the children and was more than happy to answer any questions police had for him. As the investigation progressed, police reported that Brad wasn't cooperating because he didn't go to the police station. He was also criticized for not contacting Nancy's family, for not calling police to report Nancy missing and for "selfishly" wanting his children with him instead of leaving them with Krista.

There was also a publicly televised memorial service for Nancy, and he did not want to be a part of that due to the publicity, so he was criticized for not attending that service. The service was organized by Jessica and Hannah so it's not surprising that Brad felt uncomfortable attending, knowing they were make accusations against him.

The reason Brad didn't call police immediately is because he, like most people, believed that a person had to be missing for twenty-four hours before police would assist with a search. He did what most people would do. He went out and searched for her and contacted her friends to try to track her down.

> **Tunnel vision**: the tendency of investigators to seize on an early piece of evidence that appears to implicate the defendant, and to hold on to their belief in his guilt even as other evidence points to his innocence.[1]

Jessica's accusations caused investigators to develop immediate tunnel vision, a form of confirmation bias. With confirmation bias there is a tendency to only search for things that support one's theory and ignore everything else. This is a textbook case, and it is unmistakable. The signs of this horrible phenomenon which is very common in wrongful conviction cases will be carefully outlined.

It is clear that investigators never treated this as a missing person's case. They made the assumption that Brad was responsible for Nancy's disappearance and then conducted their investigation pursuant to that belief. They immediately began building a case against Brad, but they would encounter many obstacles along the way as information and evidence pointed toward his innocence. It will be abundantly clear that they ignored the disconfirming evidence and then calculatedly fabricated evidence to create the *illusion* of facts to support their theory.

Police actions and inactions were inconsistent with what one would expect to see in a missing person's investigation. Though there were visible outward attempts to find Nancy—the National Guard flew search patterns, canine searches were sent, road blocks were set up and people were questioned, it all seemed to be for the sake of appearances.

Nancy's Cell Phone

Brad gave police Nancy's cell phone the afternoon of July 12 hoping it would assist them in finding her, but shockingly they never attempted to access it. They threw the phone in a desk for two weeks, not even placing it into evidence until July 25. The phone was password protected, but there are experts skilled in accessing phones in emergency situations. In fact, it is standard procedure for police to immediately access all of a missing person's electronic devices. They also typically review the person's recent social media usage as soon as possible, but Cary Police didn't do that either. Tunnel vision is one explanation for their failure to utilize these tools. Incompetence is another. Both are inexcusable.

Reports That Bella Saw Nancy That Morning

As mentioned, Clea Morwick was watching the two Cooper children the afternoon of July 12 while Brad talked to police. At some point Bella, who was 4 ½ at the time, told Clea that she saw her mother that morning and that she was wearing black shorts and a white t-shirt. This is important because time was critical. Police should have interviewed Bella immediately to see if she had any information about where her mother may have gone running, any plans she may have mentioned, clothing descriptions, what she ate or drank and as many details as possible while her memory was fresh.

Summary of Reports

- Bella saw Mom with black shorts and white t-shirt. Bella stated this around 5:00 p.m. (Detective Dismukes 7/12/08) [2]

- Clea told me around 5:00 p.m. today she spoke with the oldest daughter, Bella, and asked her if she saw her mommy today. Clea told me she asked Bella what her mommy was wearing when she saw her today. Clea reported Bella told her that her mommy was wearing black shorts and a white t-shirt. (Cary Police incident report, 7/12/08) [3]

- Her husband and elder child saw her leaving for her run Saturday morning. (Art2mis (Diana Duncan) (7/14/08) nancycooper.blogspot.com) [4]

Police never spoke to Bella, or if they did, it was withheld from Brad's attorneys. It was negligent for them to ignore such important information at such a critical time and it demonstrates that tunnel vision was already influencing their decisions. If they had treated it as a missing person's case, they certainly would have questioned Bella, and they also would have shared the information with the public— *"Daughter last saw her mom in black shorts and a white shirt Saturday morning . . . "*,but they chose to withhold the information.

Police Chief's Comments

While Nancy was still missing, Chief Bazemore publicly stated that this was an *isolated incident* and that joggers were safe to be out and about in the community. She all but stated that Brad was a suspect. The truth is that at that time, Cary police had no idea what had happened to Nancy. All they knew was that she was missing and that Jessica Adam had accused Brad of  harming her. Bazemore made that statement *not knowing* that it was safe for the citizens to be out. She made that statement not knowing if Jessica was a reliable source of information. It was terribly reckless and irresponsible. It was also prejudicial to Brad, who was being tried by the media.

There was a similar missing person's case in Philadelphia[5] in 2014. A woman left for a run one evening and days later was found dead. While she was a missing person and before the crime was solved, police cautioned women to be careful and to avoid running alone until the murderer was caught. Chief Bazemore, on the other hand, told the public that it was safe to be out, thus putting everyone at risk. How would it have looked if weeks or months later, investigators concluded that Brad wasn't involved in Nancy's death? It would have created an embarrassing situation for town officials. There was now extreme pressure to produce evidence that he was responsible for her death.

Bleach Rumor

During one of the press conferences, a reporter asked Chief Bazemore if she could confirm a rumor that Brad had purchased bleach at four o'clock the morning Nancy disappeared. Chief Bazemore responded that she couldn't confirm or deny the report, even though she *could* in fact deny that rumor. She already knew at that time that he purchased Tide laundry detergent, green juice and milk, and it wasn't at 4 a.m., it was between 6 and 7 a.m. She let the bleach rumor persist, and to this day some still believe Brad purchased bleach. How can this be considered anything less than malicious? It was an easy way for her to get the public on her side as she immediately began building a case against Brad. After all, it was critical to maintain Cary's safe-town image. There was even a national news story on NBC that made Brad sound guilty and that was only possible because of the conduct of Cary Police.

> "In fact, police have yet to confirm that she actually left her home that morning at 7:00 a.m. as her husband stated. Where are the witnesses, independent of her husband, who saw her leave, or enter another car, or simply walk down the street that Saturday morning?" [6]

In fact several witnesses *had* contacted police, believing that they'd seen Nancy but police remained silent. They never shared the information with the media. The prejudicial comments in the NBC article continued . . .

"Now unconfirmed reports are circulating that Brad may have purchased bleach as early as 4:00 a.m. the day Nancy was reported missing."

There wouldn't have been a bleach reference in the national story if Bazemore had responded honestly when asked about the rumor, so it's interesting to consider how the rumor began in the first place. Here's one more example to demonstrate how Bazemore's comments influenced the national media. (Continuing with the NBC News report):

Community is Safe, Police Say
Investigators have said that Nancy's murder is not believed to be a random act of violence, but an isolated incident not connected to other ongoing cases. Police also say that the local community is safe and that there is no danger to other female joggers. Question: How do you say this with such confidence unless you think you know the identity of the killer and you have the murderer under constant surveillance?[7]

In fact, police *did* have Brad under constant surveillance but never admitted they'd considered him a suspect at that point. Again, this was classic tunnel vision. They testified that they followed him for his own protection because they didn't know what had happened to Nancy. However, police did not follow the Cooper children who were in the care of other friends so that negates the claim that they followed him to ensure his safety.

Witnesses Respond to "Missing" Flyers

Flyers were posted throughout town and handed out during coordinated search efforts on Sunday and Monday, July 13 and 14. Police began receiving calls immediately from people who believed they had seen Nancy. That should have been encouraging news and a priority to immediately follow up with each person, but that did not happen. In all, sixteen people reported seeing a jogger resembling Nancy Cooper. Some were positive it was Nancy. Details from witnesses included clothing descriptions, build, hair color, specific locations, times, and even exchanged greetings. Four people provided information about a suspicious white/maroon van in the area. Oddly, none of the news reports included anything about possible sightings of Nancy or a description of the van, because police withheld that vital information.

Rosemary Zednick lived in the same Lochmere neighborhood as the Coopers. She did not know Nancy, but she was very certain she saw her that morning. She described how she was walking her dog and came face to face with Nancy as she jogged by. Rosemary said hello to her and Nancy said, "Hi," and continued jogging. When Rosemary saw the missing person flyers she became very concerned about her. In fact, she was so positive she had seen Nancy that she called police several times, but no one followed up with her.

After a couple of months had passed, Rosemary contacted Brad's defense attorneys at Kurtz and Blum to give them the information. They met with her and discussed the details and showed her a photo line-up. She readily identified Nancy.

The public became aware of Rosemary's statements about seeing Nancy when Brad's attorneys posted the information on their website. It wasn't until that time that police finally met with Rosemary. During the recorded interview, Detective Daniels told Rosemary that there were numerous witnesses who were 150% certain they saw Nancy Cooper that morning. It is astounding that they ignored the numerous sightings.

The following police reports contain the actual information received from people who believed they may have seen Nancy the morning she disappeared. Shockingly, investigators ignored the information, believing it was unimportant to follow up with them at that time. Failing to do so inhibited the possibility of finding the killer(s) because trails go cold very quickly. They wouldn't contact a single caller until three months later.

7/12/08 – 7/14/08 Sightings

"Ms. White advised that she was running on Cary Parkway around 0800 hrs when she saw a slight woman wearing a white hat, light blue top and gray shorts behind her and gaining. Ms. White advised that she turned onto Lochmere and was heading home. She did not see the other runner behind her and assumed she went straight towards Holly Springs Road." (Chris Byers, narrative #3 7/13/08)[8]

"Contacted Mike Pashby. He advised that he saw a female runner with about the same build of Ms. Cooper running south on the northbound lanes at the Kildaire Farm Rd. bridge. She was just south of the bridge when he saw her. This was around 0915-0930 hrs. Could not provide clothing description. (Chris Byers, narrative #3 7/13/08)

"Contacted Diane Castello. She advised that around 0935 hrs. she was traveling north on Kildaire Farm Rd. when she <u>saw a jogger she thought to be Ms. Cooper jogging against traffic on Kildaire Farm Rd.</u> at the bridge under construction. She advised that the jogger was wearing a <u>white shirt.</u>"(Chris Byers narrative #3 7/13/08)

"Valerie Wentzell called and stated she was jogging yesterday at approximately 810 hours jogging southbound on Kildaire near the Wendy's. I made contact with Ms. Wentzel. <u>She advised that she saw Ms. Cooper on Saturday July 12, 2008,</u> around 0810-0820 hrs. Described the jogger as a tall, thin female with a pony tail wearing shorts and a shirt. She saw her running southbound on the northbound side of Kildaire Farm Rd. (Chris Byers narrative #11 7/13/08)

"Edie Wong called to advise that she was walking her dog on the trail in the Hemlock Bluffs Nature Preserve when she <u>saw someone that looked like Ms. Cooper. She thinks that the subject was wearing a white t-shirt</u> with pink trim and that her hair was pulled back." (Chris Byers, narrative #11 – 7/13/08)

"Keith Roberts called to advise that he was walking his dog when <u>he saw someone matching Ms. Cooper's description.</u> Called and left message. Mr. Roberts called back and told dispatch that he thinks he saw the missing person on Laver Rd. East from Kildaire Farm Rd. She told him that he had a cute dog as she passed. He

also stated that he did not want anyone else to call him back."
(Chris Byers, narrative #11 – 7/13/08)

"Nancy sighter (Anthony Boone) at Fielding Drive has not seen female since 7/12. (Dismukes hand notes) [9]

"Mr. Thompson stated that he and his friend were fishing at Lake Lochmere on Saturday July 12, 2008. They were loading their fishing boat onto the trailer at the Lochmere boat ramp when they saw a female jogger on Lochmere Drive. The female was about the same height as the missing Nancy Cooper. The female was wearing a white baseball cap and white tank top. The female was running on Lochmere Drive toward Cary Parkway and she was running alone. (Mark VanHouten narrative #17 7/14/08)

"Sylvia Hink stated Saturday morning between 0700-0800 hrs. she was sitting on her front porch reading her newspaper when she noticed two white female joggers. She stated they were not jogging together and the jogger in front was wearing light blue shorts but she couldn't remember what the second jogger was wearing except something light. Hink stated Sunday morning at 0900 hrs she was walking toward the end of Fielding Drive and in the construction area when she noticed a maroon work van with two Hispanic men leaning against it as if they were not doing anything. Hink stated she left the area after that. I provided Hink with my business card and asked her to call me if she was able to think of anything else."
(Peggy Marchant narrative #32)

"Curtis Hodges called the police department to report that he may have seen the missing person this past Saturday (7/12/08) around

33

0710 hrs. He stated that he saw a female running on Kildaire Farm Rd. heading outbound and was near the golf course. <u>He stated that he saw a picture of the woman posted and is *positive* that it was her.</u> *<u>He stated that she was wearing a white top and black shorts</u>.* (Officer Joseph Lengel narrative #15 7/14/08)

"Marguerite stated on the morning of Saturday July 12, 2008, she was driving through Regency Parkway around 7:55a.m. and 8:10a.m. She stated while traveling on Regency Parkway she observed a white female with dirty blond hair wearing a baseball cap with her pony tail coming out the back.

She stated the female was wearing white shorts with maybe a tight sleeveless shirt. She advised after seeing Nancy's twin sister on television she remembered seeing the female jogger. Marguerite advised the female she saw jogging resembled Nancy Cooper, but she wouldn't say it was definitely Nancy."(Detective Dismukes report #116 7/19/08)

Beth Fenton was *certain* she saw Nancy on the morning of July 12, but by the time the detective finally spoke to her in October, it changed to *not definite*.

"At 1641 hours I spoke with Beth Fenton by telephone. Beth told me she remembered seeing Nancy Cooper jogging sometime around 9:30 a.m. on the morning of July 12th. Beth said she was working in her yard off Planters Wood Drive when she observed a <u>white female wearing a white t-shirt with black stripes going down the side. Beth stated the female was wearing black shorts</u>, white sun visor and light colored tennis shoes. She said the female's

34

height was approximately 5'7 or taller and around 120 pounds. Beth told me she was no closer than half a football field away from the jogger. She stated that she usually does not see joggers run down her street. I asked Beth if she was positive the female she saw jogging was in fact Nancy Cooper. <u>Beth told me after she saw the flyers of Nancy Cooper she was certain it was Nancy</u>. Beth followed this by telling me she would not definitely say who she saw jogging was in fact Nancy Cooper." (Detective Dismukes 10/15/08)[10]

Interestingly, one of the first Cary Police officers to arrive at the Coopers' home the day that Nancy disappeared was Officer Daniel Hayes. He reported that he saw a woman who looked like Nancy jogging in the bike lane at 7:00 a.m. while he was on patrol. This was the same location and time where Rosemary reported seeing Nancy. Officer Hayes actually wrote about this in his report after seeing a photo of Nancy at the Cooper home. He would never mention it until asked about it 2 ½ years later at trial.

"Finally I also remembered that when I first started my shift on 7/12/08 I was traveling east on Lochmere Drive about 0700. I had just passed the first lake off Lochmere when I noticed a white female runner heading west towards Lochmere Drive running in the bicycle lane. She was wearing a light blue tank top, matching shorts. Light brown hair, ponytail. At the time I thought nothing of it except wondering why is she running in the bike lane and not on the sidewalk." (Officer Hayes Cary police officer 7/12/08 narrative#7)

The reports support the likelihood that Nancy went running that morning, but they were disregarded as unimportant. The people most certain they had seen Nancy described the clothing similarly to Bella Cooper's description—white shirt, black shorts. Imagine if police had received calls from people claiming to have seen Brad that morning near Fielding Drive. Would they have ignored those witnesses?

Van Sightings

Beginning the evening of July 11, there were four independent reports about a suspicious van in the area. The descriptions weren't exact – some described a "white work truck," others described a "white and maroon van," but each person described *suspicious* activity.

Brad actually informed Detective Daniels that Nancy had mentioned an attempted abduction of a jogger from a van.

> "He stated that about two months ago Nancy told him that some-one in a van tried to kidnap a jogger. He stated that she had not been involved in this and had only heard it second hand." (Detective Daniels' narrative 7/12/08)[11]

Nancy had also mentioned something about a red van to Diana Duncan and possibly some other friends. There were email warnings between them to be careful while jogging alone.

Diana Duncan's Deposition

Q. Did Nancy ever tell you that she'd heard someone in a red van tried to abduct a female jogger?

A. It rings a bell when you say it, but I didn't remember it.[12]

36

The following accounts are described by the four witnesses. Remember that Nancy disappeared around 7 o'clock a.m. the morning of **July 12**.

<u>Jan Boyer</u> – **7/11/08 8:45 p.m.** – While walking her dog, she saw what she described as a <u>white "truck"</u> heading toward the cul-de-sac where the body would later be found. The van had <u>no headlights</u>. She noted it was odd because there was nothing back there, it was dark and the truck's headlights were off.

<u>Dale Kuerbritz</u> – **7/12/08 just past midnight** – Dale awoke to the sound of his doorbell – which would ring when his outer storm door was opened. He went to see who was there and saw a <u>white van</u> behind some bushes, then noticed someone speeding away in the van down the street at high speed, <u>lights off</u>. He called police and requested additional patrols of the neighborhood. The police were called at 12:17 a.m., so this was 3 ½ hours after Jan Boyer's sighting.

<u>Curtis Hodges</u> – **7/12/08 7:10 a.m.** – Curtis noticed a woman jogger near Lochmere Golf Course. Then he saw a van driving toward him. As it got close to the woman, it did a u-turn. When he checked his rear view mirror, there was no sign of the van, so it continued on in that direction. It did not appear to be traveling in his same direction which would have been expected in a U-turn. Later he saw the "missing" flyer of Nancy Cooper and was *positive* she was the woman he saw. By the time detectives finally talked to him, he was 90% certain it was her. The van was described as an <u>older model, reddish–white color – two Hispanic men in van.</u>

<u>Sylvia Hink</u> – **7/13/08 9:00 a.m.** Sylvia was walking in her neighborhood when she noticed a <u>maroon van</u> parked at the intersection of Belmont Forest and <u>Fielding Drive</u>. Two Hispanic men were leaning against it. She found it odd because it was a Sunday and there was no work going on in that area.

Every single encounter was suspicious. Due to the timing of the reports, combined with the information from Brad and Diana, it appeared to be a solid lead, but investigators never pursued it. They didn't meet with the four witnesses, they didn't contact the media to request public assistance in locating a van with two Hispanic drivers and they didn't alert patrol cars to be on the lookout for vehicles matching the witness's descriptions.

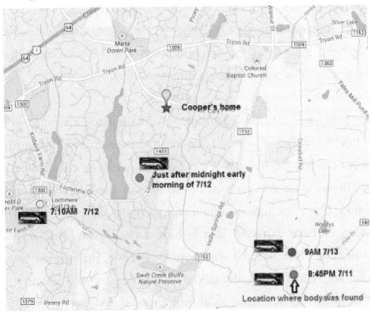

A Jan Boyer – 8:45 p.m. **July 11**
B Dale Kuerbritz – Just past midnight **July 12**

C Curtis Hodges –7:10 a.m. **July 12**
D Sylvia Hink – 9:00 a.m. **July 13**

The map depicts the location of each of the van sightings in relation to the Cooper home and the site where the body was found. Note that two of the sightings were on the same street where the body was later found and one of them was approaching the very cul-de-sac where Nancy would later be found. Tunnel vision and/or extreme negligence prevented police from trying to find the van.

Psychic-led Search

On the morning of July 13, approximately 24 hours after Nancy went missing, Detective Daniels sent three officers to the Lochmere Golf Course on a "tip" they had received from a psychic. One of Nancy's friends, Desiree Jackson, gave the detective the contact information for a psychic, Brenda Shoulders. This prompted a police search for Nancy's body in the Lochmere golf course culverts. It occurred at a time when they had already received the multiple calls from actual people who reported that they'd seen Nancy jogging. Detective Daniels didn't send any detectives to speak to those people. He was too busy following a tip from a psychic.

This was certainly a textbook case of tunnel vision and it occurred very early, before Nancy's body was even found. Police concluded that Brad had murdered Nancy after listening to the 911call. They were so certain it was true that they carelessly reported that it was not a random crime and that joggers were safe to run in the community. They ignored the early information that indicated Nancy was alive that morning – that Bella saw her mom and the many reports from people who believed they had seen her jogging. They ignored four independent reports about a strange van in the neighborhood to include the street where Nancy's body would later be found. They did this knowing that Nancy herself had recently told her husband about an attempted abduction of a jogger by someone in a van.

The failure of investigators to utilize Nancy's phone as a tool to locate her was an enormous oversight. There will be shocking information about the cell phone in a later chapter. The investigation continued in this manner, and police would have to get creative to make Brad appear guilty.

{ 6 }

Nancy's Body Is Found

William Boyer was walking his dog on Fielding Drive at approximately 7 o'clock the evening of July 14. As he approached the cul-de-sac in an undeveloped area he heard squawking and saw buzzards in the trees. He assumed it was likely a deer carcass. He continued walking and noticed what he initially thought was the deer, but as he came closer, he realized it was a human body that was visible from the street. He left the area immediately to find a phone to call 911, and first responders soon appeared at the scene. Note that this is the same location where his wife, Jan Boyer, reported seeing the suspicious white work truck heading into the very same cul-de-sac with the headlights off the night before Nancy disappeared.

Nancy's body was face down with the upper body in a *drainage pond*. The body had no clothing except for a sports bra that had been rolled under and above the breasts. Detectives Dismukes and Daniels went to the Cooper home to inform Brad that a body had been discovered, and the next day it was confirmed to be Nancy Cooper. There are a couple of things worth noting relating to the search efforts prior to the body being found. Searches were coordinated from Java Jive and Lifetime Fitness on July 13 and 14. A website was set up by Brett Adam and Diana Duncan to communicate with volunteers. Brett was Jessica's (the 911 caller who accused Brad of harming Nancy) husband. The last phone call received by Nancy the night before her disappearance was from Brett Adam's cell phone. At 12:35 p.m. on July 14, Brett posted on the website:

> "I just finished updating the **search map** we're maintaining on **Google**. It shows the areas that have been covered by volunteers reporting into both the Java Jive and Lifetime Fitness search coordination points. If you've independently searched any area, please let us know via the contact form below so that we can keep people focused on new areas that have zero coverage."

It's an interesting coincidence that Brett was utilizing Google maps for the search and Brad would later be convicted based on an alleged map search.

Brett's post continued:

> "Of course, as the police will tell you, searching twice or more is standard practice so it certainly is not a waste of effort to look again. Especially relevant *given the heavily wooded areas and many small gullies involved in much of this search area.*"

Brett specifically mentioned gullies. Nancy's body was found *in a gully*. His description of the terrain may very well have been a coincidence but it's rather odd as Cary, North Carolina, isn't exactly known for its high prevalence of gullies. Why would he specifically reference gullies when they were searching for a live person? As well, Brett Adam has a computer background and would have had the know-how to plant map files on one's computer. At 12:38 p.m., Brett posted one final time to thank volunteers and also to cancel additional searches since it had started raining. Nancy's body was found later that day.

Autopsy

The autopsy[13] was performed by Dr. John Butts on July 15, 2008. He described the death as a homicide most likely caused by asphyxiation from strangulation. There were a couple of details worth noting from the report.

> *"There is a faint linear mark across the central neck in the area of the thyroid prominence approximately 1.3" in length."*

And

"The trachea contains a small amount of fluid and debris."

This seems to indicate that she was strangled by an object such as a thin rope causing a linear mark, though the medical examiner testified at trial that there was no ligature mark. The debris found in the trachea could indicate that she was face down and while gasping for air, breathed in dirt and water. Another section of the report describes dirt caked on her knees and parts of her legs. Later, the SBI chemist examined the fingernail scrapings and also found debris under the nails. All of these things pointed to her having been killed outside, either at the location where found or any location where dirt was present. Had the medical examiner collected and analyzed the debris found in the trachea, we would have had a much better idea of the location of death, but nonetheless, the information is not consistent with the theory that she was strangled at home and then transported to the dump site (police theory). There were actually many things the examiner could have done to help determine the location and time of death, but it was not a very thorough examination or report.

After Nancy's body was discovered, Wake County/Raleigh City County Bureau of Identification (CCBI) began investigating the crime scene. Agent Hill diagrammed the location and position of the body and drew the freshest tire tracks that led directly up to the body. He also marked the position of other items found near the body—two electrical wires and a cigarette butt.

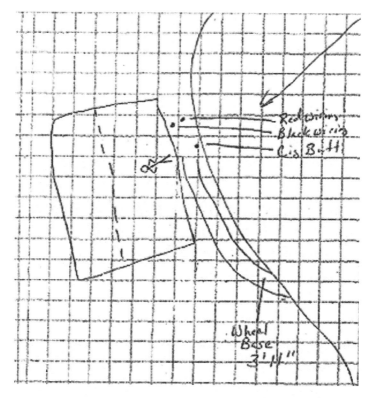

Agent Hill measured the "wheel base" by recording the distance between the two interior tracks. Both Brad's and Nancy's vehicles were compared to this measurement and were *excluded* as having made the tracks at the crime scene. The tracks were never plaster cast in an attempt to determine the type of tires or the type of vehicle that may have left them. No detailed, close-up photos were taken. At trial, Agent Hill testified that he was unable to see any tread due to the grass, but with today's technology, certainly more could have been done to identify the type of tire and vehicle. As well, with the information received about the van sightings, they should have investigated to see if the tire tracks could have been made by a vehicle of that size.

Though it's not marked on Agent Hill's sketch, there was a footprint right next to Nancy's head. Many of the first responders were walking around near the body, so there was a request to obtain all footwear of workers for elimination purposes. Oddly, that request was soon canceled and no explanation was ever provided.

Much like the tire tracks, investigators did nothing to preserve the footprints. They never poured plaster to cast the footprints for size and style determinations, they didn't measure them, and they didn't attempt to eliminate prints made by EMS workers. Visually, the prints closest to the body appeared to be small in size, certainly not consistent with Brad's size 12-13 shoe size. It is unfortunate that they didn't take efforts to preserve the footprint and tire track evidence but the fact that both pointed away from Brad Cooper should have compelled investigators to broaden the suspect list.

The wires found within inches of the body and cigarette butt right next to the tire tracks weren't sent for DNA testing until almost three years later. The wires could have potentially been used to restrain Nancy. The cigarette butt could have contained the DNA of the killer, so why didn't they send them for testing right away? The pond was off the road so nobody would have had any reason to have been driving back there and standing around smoking cigarettes in that area. No DNA profile from the cigarette butt was identified. According to the SBI, time could have been a factor. It is more likely to obtain a DNA profile when an item is tested immediately.

The sports bra and Nancy's nail scrapings were the only items remaining to potentially identify the DNA of the killer. The DNA evidence was tested by SBI Agent Ivy McMillan July 23-25, 2008. Reportedly no DNA was found, not even a fragment of anyone's DNA. Surprisingly, even Nancy's DNA was absent from her nail scrapings and the bra that she was wearing. The scrapings did test positive for the presence of blood.

On July 29, Amanda Thompson of the SBI reviewed Agent McMillan's results. Three days later, Thompson met with Cary Police detectives to review the results. At that time DNA samples were requested from the Cooper children. DNA would typically be requested only for elimination purposes. For unknown reasons, Cary Police never did obtain the children's DNA.

On August 18, 2008, nail scrapings were tested a second time, and the entire sample was consumed, leaving the defense no opportunity to have a sample independently tested; thus lessening Brad's ability to prove his innocence. The reported result again was that no DNA was found.

Agent McMillan analyzed the vaginal swabs for presence of sperm, and they were negative. The prosecution indicated that this was verification that no sexual assault had occurred. *Dateline NBC* stated the same thing, "There was no sign of sexual assault." However, McMillan admitted under cross examination that it is possible that the sample was too degraded to identify sperm the same way she explained that the nail samples and bra cuttings were too degraded to yield any DNA. As well, there could have been sexual assault with the perpetrator wearing a condom. Thus, it is impossible to know whether or not sexual assault (or consensual sex) occurred before Nancy was killed.

In 2010, an independent audit of the North Carolina SBI revealed that crime lab analysts were routinely withholding more sensitive blood tests that were exculpatory to defendants. There were over two hundred reported cases.[14] The Cooper investigation occurred in 2008, so it's difficult to trust the results in light of the scandal; however, there is nothing that can be done about it. Unless the case is reopened, there will never be another review of the evidence and how it was handled.

{ 7 }

Police Theory

Detective Daniels

Detective Young

The detectives assigned to investigate the murder of Nancy Cooper were Lead Detective George Daniels, Detective Adam Dismukes and Detective Jim Young. They theorized that Brad strangled Nancy when she returned home from the party shortly after midnight, that he removed her dress, dressed her in only a sports bra to make it appear as though she was assaulted while jogging, and then transported her body to Fielding Drive. They speculated that since Brad was a Voice over IP expert he "must have" automated a phone call to make it appear as if Nancy called while he was on his way to the store. It wouldn't be until two months later that the Google map files were found, so up until that point, they had absolutely nothing to substantiate their theory. If you take away the Google search, there's no case left at all.

In order for this scenario to work, everything would have to work perfectly and Brad would have had to devise this plan in advance—a very risky plan. Consider the vulnerabilities in the police detectives' theory. The "murder plan" would have consisted of Brad's pulling his car into the garage in the middle of the night to place the body in the trunk, hoping he would not leave a trace of evidence or wake the neighbors or his daughters with the noise. The plan would also include leaving his daughters home alone three times—first to get rid of the body and then two more times with the trips to the store to set up an alibi. There would be the risk that they would wake up, become terrified at being alone, and more risk that they would possibly inform someone that they were alone. There would be the risk of neighbors seeing him driving away from the home or arriving back at an odd hour. He would have to hope that no one on Fielding Drive noticed his car on that road sometime that morning. He would risk getting a flat tire, tracking dirt from the dump location, getting a traffic ticket, or getting into a car accident. There is also a risk that the spoofed call wouldn't work or would be identified with some type of record. If any one of these things occurs, his plan falls apart and he's certain to face life in prison or even the death penalty. We're to believe that this is the best plan an intelligent engineer could come up with?

Is it even logical that he would decide to dress her in only a bra? If he wanted to make it look like she went running, why not just dress her in her full running clothing? What's even more ridiculous is the idea that an IT expert who works with computers all day long just happened to carelessly look at Fielding Drive on his work computer and leave the files there. There are computer labs all throughout Cisco, but he decided, "Hey, I think I'm going to take a look at Google maps on my own laptop computer to find a location to dump a body, even though the maps are always outdated by at least a year. Sure, that's a good plan." It just isn't plausible.

In future chapters it will become clear that police had absolutely nothing to support their theory, so they manipulated witnesses to provide them with statements to support their theory, and they fabricated evidence to bolster their very weak case against Brad. Specifically, they would often consult with Jessica Adam and Hannah Prichard, the two women who were most strongly pointing the finger at Brad. It was astounding to see the lengths police went through to build a case out of nothing. Every aspect of the investigation was touched by incompetence and deception.

{ 8 }

Time of Death Determination

There were four types of evidence available to determine the time-of-death – blood alcohol content, caffeine level, stomach contents and entomology specimens. A careful analysis was important because there was so little evidence to work with in this case. Would the evidence point to a time of death consistent with the state's timeline – shortly after midnight, or with Brad's timeline—after 7 a.m.?

The medical examiner, Dr. Butts, noted that the time of death was "consistent with the period of time interval she was reported missing." She was reported missing just after 7 a.m., so this was consistent with what Brad told police. However, Cary police convinced the doctor to shift the window all the way back to "sometime after midnight." Officer Grier faxed a letter to Dr. Butts and incorrectly informed him that Nancy Cooper was last seen shortly after midnight, totally ignoring the fact Brad reported seeing her at 7 a.m.

"The information we had concerning when Mrs. Cooper was last seen alive was around 12:30 a.m. Saturday morning, July 12th, 2008." (letter from Cary Police to Dr. Butts, July 17, 2008)

Detective Young spoke with Dr. Butts approximately a week later, on July 23. His handwritten notes reflect the time of death window to include a time from midnight to 7a.m.

- Time of death – <u>decomp. of body consistent with Nancy being seen last @ 7 am on July 12</u>
- Could be anytime b/w 12AM – 7 AM
- On July 12th – no way to set exact time of death based on decomp.

(Detective Young's hand notes)

These notes are totally contradictory! It appears that Dr. Butts really wanted to place the time of death after seven o'clock a.m., but was swayed into backing it up to "after midnight." Dr. Butts' trial testimony also leaned more strongly toward a time of death after 7 a.m., but that midnight-to-seven window remained as prosecutors pressed him. Note that it is typical for investigators to manipulate medical examiners into extending the time of death window to fit their theory.

Q. And did you attempt to make a determination of – or can you make a determination of the time of death based on your findings?
A. Yes. I offered an opinion as to the date of death.
Q. Okay. And what was that opinion?
A. I concluded, based on the condition of her remains that she'd been dead <u>for the period of time that she was reported missing</u>.

Q. And is that – is it also consistent with her – while – she was reported missing in the early morning hours of the 12th of July; is that correct?

A. That's my understanding, yes, sir.

Q. So are your findings also consistent with her death having occurred as much as twelve hours before or after that?

A. Yes, sir. Again, <u>there's a window.</u> The overall condition of the remains, though, is certainly, in my opinion, consistent with her having been dead or dying on or about the 12th.

Blood Alcohol Level

Dr. Butts obtained blood from the chest cavity and determined that the blood alcohol level was 60 mg/dl (or .06). He testified that this level was *consistent with decomposition alone.* Since witnesses from the party confirmed that Nancy had consumed several glasses of wine and a few beers that night, with estimates up to as many as 10 drinks, the low alcohol level was much more consistent with the death occurring after 7 a.m., when she would have had ample time to metabolize the alcohol.

When a person dies with alcohol in their system, the alcohol doesn't have a chance to be metabolized; so according to the state's theory, the level should have been much higher than 0.06. Based on the number of drinks Nancy reportedly consumed, if an estimated BAC level of .16 is used, and Nancy died at 12:15 a.m., the BAC should have been at least 0.22%. The state accounted for this by suggesting that Nancy "could have" vomited while being strangled, thus lowering that figure to what the medical examiner reported, .06%. It was the only explanation offered to account for the low alcohol level, but what makes much more sense is that Nancy went to sleep when she returned from the party and was able to metabolize the alcohol.

Interestingly, two samples from the body were obtained for BAC – one from the pleural cavity and one from the liver. The liver result was never reported and it is unknown why the test results were missing. That could have provided additional information to determine a more accurate time of death.

Stomach Contents

Dr. Butts determined that Nancy's stomach was virtually empty, aside from a small amount of reddish liquid and a tiny piece of what appeared to be an onion. Guests reported that Nancy ate ribs, avocado salad and cake that evening, and it was after Brad and the girls had gone home at 8 p.m. It takes an average of four to six hours to digest a medium-sized meal. Protein can take even longer to digest. If Nancy ate between the hours of 8:00 p.m. and midnight, and then died soon after returning home, she should have had some undigested food remaining in her stomach at the time of the autopsy. The empty stomach is therefore much more consistent with Nancy being alive after 7 a.m. This would have allowed time for all the food to be completely digested. Again, the prosecution's explanation was that she "could have" vomited up the food. There was no evidence to support that claim, because the dress she wore to the party had no trace of any vomit.

Caffeine

The toxicology screen detected the presence of caffeine in Nancy's system. Friends and family described how she would typically drink coffee in the morning before a run and that she would not eat anything until afterward. This was another problem for investigators, because it too pointed toward Nancy being alive that morning. How could they account for the caffeine in her system? Police spoke to all the guests who attended the Duncans' party the night before to inquire about caffeinated drinks—was soda available? Was coffee served? No, there were no caffeinated drinks served. After nothing turned up there, Detective Dismukes questioned Hannah Prichard about the food and drinks Nancy consumed at lunch time on July 11.

"After talking with Diana, I called Hannah Prichard to see what Nancy may have eaten while they were at the pool together." (Detective Dismukes (8/28/08))[15]

"Nancy had a sandwich from Village Deli – turkey, avacodo, lettuce and tomato, jalapenos, guacamole." "Food and drinks Friday day time July 11, at pool."(Detective Dismukes) [16]
Note: no mention of any caffeinated drinks.

"At 9:00 p.m. Hannah called and said she spoke with Susan Crook, who was also at the pool on July 11. Susan said she was positive Nancy was drinking a **diet coke** at the pool and had turkey on her sandwich, maybe with wheat bread."(Detective Dismukes)[17]

Did Detective Dismukes inform Hannah that they needed to identify a source of caffeine, other than a morning cup of coffee? Why would she have called him that evening to inform him about the Diet Coke if she didn't know the significance? At trial, the alleged Diet Coke was the only caffeine Nancy "may" have consumed, although it is doubtful that she would have had a soda. According to Brad, the Coopers didn't typically purchase soda and he is unaware of Nancy drinking soda but I suppose its "possible" she drank a Diet Coke that day. The more likely scenario is that she drank coffee before her run on Saturday morning, but this case was all about "could haves," and they stretched things any way possible to fit their theory.

Entomology Specimens

Agent Hill (the same agent who neglected to cast the tire tracks and foot prints at the scene) was also responsible for collecting entomology specimens. Typically specimens are collected from all areas of and nearby the body but in this case they only collected specimens from the head, or at least that is all that was reported. The specimens are then supposed to be properly labeled and preserved.

There were problems with the way both the preserved and live specimens were handled. Some specimens need to be killed and preserved immediately so the sizes of the larvae are locked in. Others are kept alive with a food source so that they grow to adult size and a species can be determined. Both are important in determining time of death. Though a food source was used to sustain the *live* specimens, they were sealed in an airtight jar and placed in a locker for two weeks before being sent to the entomologist, Dr. David Wesley Watson, and as a result, very few specimens survived. This was sheer negligence on the part of Agent Hill.

The *preserved* specimens were immediately placed in alcohol. That wasn't the best way to handle them because it causes the specimens to shrivel and change color. They should have been dipped in hot water for 30 seconds and *then* placed in the alcohol or alternatively they could have been dipped in KAA solution (mixture of kerosene, glacial acetic acid and denatured alcohol) to kill them and then placed in ethyl or isopropyl alcohol. As a result of the mishandling of both types of specimens, Dr. Watson didn't have much to work with. The limited number of samples combined with temperature variations in larval

58

development made it difficult to pinpoint the time of death. His testimony did not contribute anything toward the determination of time of death.

<u>Dr. Watson's Trial Testimony</u>:

Q. Can you make the conclusion that eggs were deposited on Ms. Cooper's body before daylight on July 12th, or are you unable to, based on the data that you have?

A. I would not estimate that. I can't make that assertion.

Dr. Watson testified that there was a large maggot mass on the back of Nancy's head, typically consistent with trauma. He stated that he later learned that there was no sign of trauma noted during the autopsy. It is therefore unclear why the insects would have accumulated in this area of the body. It is possible there was in fact trauma at the back of her head, missed by the medical examiner. It is also interesting that he received the samples and did the testing in July and August 2008 but did not issue his report until June 2010. The reason for the delay is unclear.

It seemed obvious that the strategy of the prosecution was to confuse the jury by eliciting meaningless testimony to make it appear that there was something there. They spent a great deal of time questioning the witness about very detailed descriptions of each state of larvae development and other difficult to follow (and very boring) specifics about insects, but ultimately the conclusion was that time of death could not be reported with any accuracy. He could have gotten to the point within minutes instead of hours, and really there was no point in even calling this witness, as he did not provide any conclusive results.

It's important to point out that Brad Cooper was dependent on the proper handling of all evidence to increase his abilities to prove his innocence, and once again they failed him. There were several investigative insufficiencies in the handling of evidence related to time of death determination in this case.

- A more accurate caffeine analysis could have provided data about the length of time the caffeine was in Nancy's system.

- The conspicuously absent liver analysis for alcohol could have offered a better determination of time of death.

- Had the entomology specimens been properly handled, they may have been able to offer proof that time of death had to have been after 7 a.m., ruling Brad out as a suspect.

- CCBI did not collect insects from the soil near the body. That could have indicated whether or not the body had been moved after death.

- Specimens collected from other areas of the body could have determined whether or not sexual assault occurred.

It was easy for investigators to mishandle the evidence, thus reducing Brad's ability to prove his innocence. This is unfortunately common because it helps the investigator's build their theory. There are so many CSI techniques available today, but if investigators believe that the results will be inconsistent with their theory, it is convenient to state that the evidence was inconclusive. However, the overall evidence pointed much more strongly toward the death occurring after 7 a.m. than the State's timeline of "just after midnight."

{ 9 }

Nancy's Exaggerations Impact the Case

Nancy Cooper had a tendency to embellish stories and seemed to enjoy the attention she received. She would often modify the tales over time, adding drama to make them sound more interesting and as a result different people received variations of any given story. There were several instances of this, and they spanned many topics—money issues, Brad's affair, health issues, and all types of other everyday occurrences. For the most part, the stories were harmless, but after she died, the exaggerated stories were used by police to build a case against Brad. The stories fueled the tunnel vision phenomenon described earlier, as police latched onto specific versions of stories that painted Brad in a negative light, even when they were known to be false. They in turn disregarded the versions that were favorable to Brad – even when verified to be true. The claims were presented to the District Attorney's office without providing the totality of information received.

Many witnesses described Nancy's tendencies to exaggerate

"Nancy often exaggerated the details of stories for dramatic effect. For example, if we all went to a hotel and there was a small indoor pool, when we got back, Nancy would tell people it was an Olympic sized pool and that it had diving boards. She liked to tell people stories and liked the attention." (Scott Heider's affidavit)

"And I think it's really important to understand that if you were to talk to any of the friends who've known her longer, you know, um, Laura Hiller, uh Carrie Dittner, that everybody would tell you that she had what we call a 'Nancyism,' where . . . you know, I think I've said it before, if we can all agree that these walls are pretty much gray, that she would . . . you know, depending on her audience, say, 'Wow, I went into this office and it was brilliant. It was a corner office and an all glass building and it was 20 feet tall and . . .' you know, it depended on what would be more impressive to somebody. And I said it before; that I never considered it to be malicious. It was more that she needed to feel important." (Detective Dismukes interview with Heather Metour 7/29/08) [18]

"Nancy embellished the truth at times." (Paul and Carrie Dittner 8/8/08)

To further illustrate Nancy's mindset, she created a story about a health issue during the fall of 2007. The Coopers were going to have a new home built, and Nancy sent their real estate agent, Tom Garrett, an email stating that they would have to back out of the contract because she had pneumonia and thought she might have a growth on her lung. Nancy later told a few friends the same story but expanded it to include a required biopsy procedure.

<u>12/9/07 email from Carrie to Nancy</u>
Carrie: "Hey, what happened with your x-ray?"
Nancy: "There is still a growth and it will most likely need to be biopsied. They are sending my results to a specialist to see. I will let you know."

There is no information in any of the insurance or medical records about any diagnosis or treatments for pneumonia and nothing about a need for a biopsy. This demonstrates Nancy's strong need for attention and her effortless ability to make up stories.

Hannah and Jessica are the only people who never acknowledged that Nancy would embellish and exaggerate, and those were the two people police went to anytime they had a question throughout the investigation. Again, tunnel vision guided police. They went to the people who were most likely to provide information that supported their theory. As a result, police didn't receive complete and accurate information, and in fact the stories from these women and others evolved over time and were molded to fit the police theory, but there will be more about that later.

Friendship Backgrounds
<u>Jessica Adam</u>
Nancy met Jessica Adam at their children's daycare in the summer of 2006. At the time, Nancy was best friends with Heather Metour, and they were practically inseparable. Jessica didn't like Heather, and she sensed that Heather didn't really like Nancy bringing a new friend

around. Jessica described how she was *desperate* to be friends with Nancy, but Heather prevented them from getting as close as Jessica would have liked. [19]

Sometime in the spring of 2007, there was a rift in the friendship, and Jessica asked Nancy to return everything she had ever given her, including furnishings, children's clothing, toys, and gifts. Jessica also returned everything to Nancy that she had given her. She described it as an uncomfortable situation for both of them but explained that they got past it and maintained their friendship. What could have precipitated the falling out?

There was another incident that caused bad feelings in the spring of 2008. A large group went out for drinks and dancing to celebrate a birthday. At one point one of the women, Michelle Simmons, showed Jessica a text message received on Nancy's phone. The message was from "Brett." Michelle said, "Jessica, why is your husband texting Nancy?" Jessica became very upset and even broke into tears. Nancy then also became upset and threw her phone. Jessica eventually learned that the text was actually from Brett Wilson, Nancy's former boyfriend, before she began dating Brad. Naturally the incident was embarrassing for Jessica, but it's unclear how upset she may have been. Perhaps she felt betrayed by Nancy and perceived it as them making a joke at her expense.

In the weeks prior to Nancy's death, the two women spent a lot of time together. Nancy painted Jessica's house the Tuesday and Wednesday before her disappearance to earn extra money. When Nancy disappeared, Jessica acted oddly, of course, with the hysterical 911 call, the accusations against Brad, yelling at the neighbors and inconsistent statements, but one of the oddest things she did occurred shortly after Nancy's body was found. She called Brad and asked him for Nancy's Ella Moss dress that she had worn to the Duncans' party the night before she died. Brad told her Nancy had spilled wine on the dress, so she didn't ever get it and the dress would end up being collected into evidence, but the request for the dress was very odd.

Hannah Prichard

Hannah told police she and Nancy were best friends, told each other everything, and saw each other every day.

> "Um, I've known Nancy, uh, almost two years. She and I instantly became best friends. We spent every day together. We were each other's number one and literally spent every single day together." (Hannah Prichard interview with Detective Dismukes 7/22/08)[20]

The truth is that Nancy and Hannah had only been friends for thirteen months at the time of Nancy's death. Hannah seemed to mischaracterize the friendship level as she wasn't really with her every day. For example, Nancy was painting at Jessica's Tuesday and Wednesday that week and wasn't with Hannah. Nancy went on a trip to Washington, D.C., with friends in January 2008, and Hannah did not go. Jessica and Hannah didn't even know about Nancy's affairs, or if they did, they did not share the information with police. There will be more about this in a later chapter.

It's important to note Nancy's tendencies to exaggerate for the sole reason that the stories became a big part of the case. Just weeks before trial, the State filed a hearsay exception motion requesting that all of Nancy's statements to friends and family should be included in the trial. The judge granted the request. Remember that he denied the defense request for Bella's statements about seeing Nancy the morning she disappeared but he allowed the exaggerated, false stories. This was extremely unfair.

Hearsay

Q. What is "hearsay", and why is it usually not accepted?

A. One type of evidence that usually is not allowed by the rules of evidence is "hearsay." Hearsay is what might be called "second-hand" evidence. It usually involves a witness testifying not about what he or she personally saw or heard but to establish as a fact something someone else told the witness. Hearsay evidence is generally not admissible because it may place crucial evidence before the court without allowing the other side to confront the person who is being quoted to challenge the accuracy of the statement or the credibility of the person who made it. The concept is similar to anonymous Internet posts. Information from an unknown or unavailable source is not worth much at all.[21]

The prosecution refused to acknowledge Nancy's tendency to exaggerate stories for attention. Like police, they wanted to use the information against Brad, whether it was true or not. Nancy's statements were cherry picked to bolster their case. They highlighted the damaging, yet untrue, statements and ignored the facts that refuted the statements. They did this dozens of times.

One of the more popular claims was that Brad would follow Nancy to the gas station and fill up her tank with only enough gas for her to drive to the store or to take the kids to school. Many of her friends referenced the baseless claim in their affidavits written for Nancy's family in the custody case.

"Instead of Brad giving Nancy money to put gas in her car, he would follow her to the gas station and use his credit card. Brad had a pretty tight leash on Nancy." (Diana Duncan) [22]

"Instead, Brad started escorting her to the gas station in order to use his ATM card to fill her car. He would only fill it with as much gas as he deemed necessary for the bare minimum of travel needed for getting the kids to and from school and for getting to and from the grocery store." (Brett Adam)

In this instance, Detective Daniels flat-out lied to Hannah Prichard when he told her that Brad stated he would follow Nancy to the gas station. This was untrue. Brad never made that statement. Hannah didn't seem to be aware of Brad following Nancy to the gas station.

Detective Daniels: And now, on the same subject, when she would need gas, he said he would go with her to get gas. Is that normal that . . . did she tell you about that?
Hannah: Um, maybe that happened on occasion.
Detective Daniels: Usually she'd have to use it out of the $300?
Hannah: Right. I mean I remember many instances where, you know, she would just get in the car with me because she would have like 8 miles left in her tank. (7/22/08 interview with Hannah Prichard)

Note that police are legally permitted to lie to suspects during interrogations in an effort to obtain information, but it's unclear if they are allowed to lie to witnesses to try to obtain statements that support their theory. It certainly seems improper. Brad successfully refuted the claims in his affidavit. He had credit card statements showing the two occasions when he purchased gas for Nancy. On one occasion he filled the tank and on another occasion he topped off her tank in preparation for her vacation with her parents and sister.

"Jessica Adam and Brett Adam state that when I filled up Nancy's BMW X5 I did not fill it up completely. There were two occasions where I did fill up her car myself, and on both occasions I did completely fill the tank. On May 22, 2008, I put $98.54 worth of gas into her SUV. On June 28 when Nancy was preparing to meet her family for a week-long vacation, I vacuumed, scrubbed and cleaned her car then topped up the gas tank with $59.30 worth of gas." (Brad Cooper affidavit 7/24/08)

If the stories about Brad following Nancy to the gas station had any basis, the credit card statements would have reflected several small gasoline purchases, but investigators never acknowledged concrete evidence that supported Brad's versions of the stories. The jury heard from multiple witnesses that Brad followed Nancy to the gas station so that he could limit her fuel. It wasn't true.

"Water Was Cut Off"

Nancy told some friends that Brad intentionally cut off the water from the home; she told others that he simply forgot to pay the bill, and when she really felt like adding drama, she described how he "cut the water off at the street." This is another great example to demonstrate the tactics of police and prosecutors. They only needed to look at the Coopers' water statements. The cut-off notice stated that service was suspended due to non-payment, but instead they clung to the dramatic stories.

The water bill was actually overdue several times that year, but Nancy didn't share that detail with her friends. The actual billing record showed five late payments and two reconnect fees. Nancy used the February cut-off to create a story that portrayed Brad as controlling. She had recently learned of the affair and was possibly trying to win an upper hand in the divorce. She naturally was upset that the water was cut off. That part was true, but Brad did not intentionally miss the payment due to control or spite.

Statements to police:
"Diana says Brad failed to pay water bill and unconcerned about the effect on children."[23]

"Brad began to retaliate by shutting off the water and canceling credit cards." (Jessica Adam 7/12/08) [24]

"Brad at one point cut the water off at the house."(Hannah Prichard, 7/15/08)[25]

"For example, she told me one time that she got up in the morning and the water was shut off in the house, with two young kids. And she said she called him at work and said, 'Hey, we don't have any water.' He said, 'Well I turned it off at the street. I just wanted you to know that I can do that. I'll turn it back on maybe when I get home tonight.'" (Interview with Tom Garrett 9/04/08)[26]

Nancy told her longer term friend, Carrie Dittner, the truth.

"Carrie told me she heard on the news that the Coopers' water was turned off because Brad did not pay the bill because he was trying to teach Nancy a lesson. She stated this was not true because Nancy told her their water had been turned off because they forgot to pay the water bill. Carrie followed this by stating that Nancy embellished the truth at times."[27] (Detective Dismukes interview 8/8/08)

Nancy's story gained momentum when one of Hannah Prichard's friends, Susan Crook, actually contacted Interact to report the incident on Nancy's behalf. Interact is an agency that assists women who are in abusive relationships. Susan testified at Brad's trial that she tried to convince Nancy to call Interact but she refused, so she placed a call herself. If the water-cut-off story were true, wouldn't Nancy have wanted to contact Interact herself? Would Nancy have agreed to give Brad joint custody of the girls if he was dangerous enough to cut the water off out of spite? It's unlikely. Brad was asked about the water being cut off during his custody deposition.

Brad Cooper Custody Deposition, 10/02/08:
Q. Was there ever an occasion in early 2008 when either your water or utilities were cut off?
A. Yes, late February. We missed paying a bill and missed the cancellation notice, and they shut off our water for one day.
Q. When you say "we" who normally paid the household bills?
A. I guess I would – I would normally pay them online.
Q. Okay. What caused you to miss the bill and miss the cancellation notice?

A. We had bills scattered all over most of the home. The front desk, the desk in the living room, we had bills upstairs. A lot of them were unopened, so it's – it's one that I didn't grab from the mailbox. Our mail comes in the afternoon. Nancy usually picks up the mail in the afternoon and puts it in the house.

Q. And how did Nancy react when the water was turned off?

A. She was pretty upset. You know, I mean you couldn't – you couldn't wash clothes, you couldn't do dishes. So she contacted me, and I immediately contacted the Town of Cary to have it turned on that day.

Q. Did she blame you for that?

A. I believe yeah, she probably blamed me. Yes.

So a simple thing like the water being cut off for a day was twisted and used to portray Brad as a controlling husband. It painted an inaccurate picture of the Coopers' relationship. Another example was a story about Nancy having to walk everywhere because Brad wouldn't buy her a car. The truth was they were waiting to get her the exact car that she wanted – a BMW X5.

"Brad refused to buy Nancy a car, yet he drove a BMW. Nancy was forced to walk with Bella to the doctor, grocery store, etc." (Hannah Prichard's affidavit)

"Brad did not provide Nancy with a car the first year they were in North Carolina." (Desiree Jackson's affidavit)

Brad's Rebuttal:

"Hannah Prichard states that I refused to buy Nancy a car. The truth is that Nancy would not permit us to purchase her new vehicle for her unless it was a BMWX5. The vehicle needed to be silver or white in color and have the rear climate package. On numerous occasions we met with Roland Lewis at Leith BMW and looked at available certified pre-owned BMW X5's. The vehicles we found either did not match Nancy's specifications or were priced beyond what we could afford. I suggested numerous times that we look at selling our BMW 325 and purchasing two more affordable cars, but Nancy stated she earned her X5 and wouldn't settle for anything else. For a short time, a few months, we shared a single vehicle where I sometimes had Nancy drive me to work. I carpooled, I took the bus or I brought the car to work. The BMW 325 was actually her car and was purchased for her when she was pregnant with Bella in 2004."[28]

Mike Hiller corroborated Brad's account.

"And then she said that she's waiting for a very specific car to be available on this preferred pre-owned BMW. And so it's her choice that they don't have a car and she could go out and have any car but if she wanted this BMW she would have to wait." (Mike Hiller 7/30/08)[29]

Nancy did get her BMW X5 as soon as a model that met her specifications became available, but the State elicited testimony about all of the false, dramatic stories through multiple witnesses at trial. They were only able to do it because Judge Gessner allowed the hearsay. This was not typical to allow this type of information because it was secondhand and not verifiable. It was prejudicial, and it was unethical for prosecutors to elicit statements based on falsehoods. The Defense was able to counter the stories when they called their own witnesses, but by that time the jury was worn down, and it's unclear how much information they were able to absorb. There are many other similar examples – claims that Nancy had no means to open a bank account, had her allowance cut after she earned money painting, had her cell phone taken away, but there are more important things to discuss about this case. Understand that these examples were all the same. They were baseless claims based on Nancy's stories that she told friends to get attention, and they were easily refuted.

Finances

Nancy also exaggerated information about her financial status to friends, so some background is necessary. By 2007, the Coopers were living beyond their means. They had trouble keeping up with the bills, accumulated massive credit card debt, borrowed against Brad's 401K, and maxed out their home equity line of credit. Both Brad and Nancy spent a lot of money, but that year in particular, Nancy charged $27,000 of the $40,000 balance on their American Express card. Status was important to her, and her friends described how she often shopped at *Uniquities*, a designer clothing store. She bought wine at $15-20 a bottle and had grown accustomed to living beyond their means. Her friends' statements described her love of spending.

- "Nancy had expensive tastes – shopped a lot. Nancy drank more than most – bottle of wine." (Diana Duncan) [30]

- "Nancy did sometimes spend a lot of money on shopping." (Hannah Prichard 7/15/08) [31]

- "Brad always gave Nancy everything that she wanted such as designer clothing, wine and jewelry." (Scott Heider)

- "Nancy had expensive taste; she 'bought freely,' created financial stress. Nancy commented she was on allowance. Carrie says Nancy was not deprived." (Detective Dismukes notes)[32]

The Coopers could no longer sustain this level of spending, so in the early part of 2008, Brad consulted with a financial planner and devised a budget to rein in spending; however, Nancy continued to overdraw the bank account, so a weekly cash allowance became necessary. The budget was very generous. After all bills were paid including mortgage, utilities, car payments, pool and gym memberships, Nancy would have three hundred dollars cash per week for food and household items. Brad wasn't strict with the budget, and if Nancy wanted something special that exceeded the allowance, Brad often found a way to buy it for her. When Nancy traveled, Brad gave her additional spending money.

Nancy's budget was a sore spot. She often complained to family and friends that she didn't have enough money even though bank records verify that she received three hundred dollars each week. Nancy referred to Brad as a "budget Nazi" to friends. By the time of the custody hearing, the stories had become so extreme that Nancy was described as a mother who didn't have enough money to feed her children, and it simply was not true.

- "Every Sunday Brad gave her $300 to cover gas, food and any specific needs for the girls. When she would buy food Brad would eat it. As a result, there wasn't any food for her and the girls. It just wasn't enough." (Jennifer Fetterolf 7/23/08)[33]

- "Approximately January of 2008, Brad began to restrict Nancy's access to money. Nancy said he gave her $50 and said, 'make it work.'" (Desiree Jackson) [34]

- "Brad would give Nancy limited cash every week for groceries but at times would still refuse to pay her, making her beg him to go buy diapers because she had no way to buy them." (Hannah Prichard)

Nancy told friends the budget was anywhere from fifty dollars per week, to the actual amount of three hundred dollars, again because she liked to exaggerate. Kinde Rawlins told police that she had heard stories that Nancy didn't have money, but that was inconsistent with everything she'd seen. Nancy managed to purchase a dress at an upscale clothing boutique just two days before her disappearance . . . all the while complaining to friends and family that she didn't have any money. Obviously, that wasn't true.

Kinde Rawlins interview with Detective Dismukes 7/28/08
A. She knew how to push his buttons. We all know how to push our husband's buttons. Um, she spent a lot of money. That's the thing that is weird to me is that there's so much talk about how she didn't have any money. She said she didn't have access to money, but she had access to credit cards? It doesn't seem right to me, because I have a friend that I work with who has a friend that works at *Uniquities*, which is the Cameron Village boutique.
Q. Um hmm.
A. And she said she looked up the last receipt and it was that Thursday before that Saturday she went missing.
Q. Um hmm.

A. She spent a lot of money at one time. I can't remember how much it was, so I don't even want to say.

Q. That was through a credit card though from what you . . .

A. Well, I don't know. I mean, I would imagine so since she didn't have any money. Where . . . how else is she gonna . . .

Q. Right.

A. But then I'm like, did she not have money or did she . . . I don't . . . the whole thing is very . . . I don't know. When she came to Trader Joe's, she had a cartload of food.[35]

At one point in 2007, Nancy told her friends that she was spending money to punish Brad for the affair. In particular, she purchased a painting of a bear for a sum of $9,000. She charged it to her credit card, even though Brad had told her they could not afford it. This shows her inability to control her spending impulses. Hannah Prichard told Detective Dismukes that Nancy bought the painting to get back at Brad for the affair, and others repeated the same statement to police. [36]

The truth is that Nancy purchased the bear painting months before she learned of the affair, but after she learned of the affair, she decided to tell everyone that she bought it to "punish" Brad for the affair. Police tried to use this as evidence that Brad was upset about the purchase and that it provided motive for murder. However, there is no indication that Brad was excessively angry about it. Hannah told Detective Dismukes that Brad joked about being tired of seeing the recurring credit card statements for the painting.

"He was mad. I mean I remember him actually *making a joke* about how he's really tired of getting these charges." (7/22/08) [37]

Detective Dismukes twisted Hannah's expression in his narrative.

"According to Hannah, Brad was extremely upset after Nancy bought the painting." (Detective Dismukes)[38]

Police would often record hand notes and then later type up a narrative with an emotion or statement never conveyed by the witness. "making a joke" was translated to "extremely angry."

During opening arguments, the defense described how Nancy planned to hurt Brad in the divorce by making it appear that she was not given enough money to survive. Her friends, Doug and Pam Letts called her on it when she got caught up in her own lies.

Excerpt from defense opening statements at trial

"Doug Letts has unique insight into just how those stories were developed. Doug was married to Pam Letts one of Nancy's friends. In late 2007, after a bottle of wine, Nancy told Pam that she had a plan. Nancy said that she was going to spend Brad into submission while at the same time telling her friends that Brad wasn't giving her enough money for food and that she was forced to borrow money from friends so that she could pay bills.

"A couple of months after that initial conversation, over another glass of wine, Nancy told Doug and Pam about how Brad wasn't giving her enough money for food, and Doug said, 'Nancy, I know that's not true. You just told us that's what you were gonna be doing. You just told us that's what you were gonna be telling people.' Nancy laughed. She told him, 'Shut up.' And they forgot about it. What started as Nancy getting the upper hand in a divorce was now woven into the fabric of the custody battle and murder investigation."

There are indications that Nancy did exactly what was described by the Letts's. She did tell several friends and family members that she had barely enough money to survive, but she failed to include the fact that their financial strains were a result of excessive spending. Nancy didn't tell any of her friends that they had to take out a second mortgage and borrow from Brad's 401K just to make ends meet.

Brad gave Nancy seven hundred dollars cash to for her vacation with her family in July. Instead of conserving the cash and making it last for the whole trip, she bought food for everyone at the house the first day of the trip and quickly burned through all of her cash. She was then reliant on her family to pick up the tab for the rest of the trip as she told them that she had run out of cash.

At the end of the vacation, her father gave her money for an electric toothbrush that she said she couldn't afford, and her sister also gave her some cash. The day after she arrived home, she spoke to her father and told him that she had to spend the toothbrush money on an exterminator bill because payment was required at the time of the service. The truth is the exterminator, Gary Beard, testified that he did not demand payment that day and was fine with allowing the Coopers to pay at a later time.

Aside from alleged financial control, there was an implication that Brad kept constant tabs on Nancy. The reality was that Nancy could come and go as she pleased. She took a trip to Washington, D.C., with friends in January 2008. She went on a beach trip with a male friend of the couple's, Mike Morwick and the children. Few spouses would be agreeable to such a trip. She also spent the week in Hilton Head with her family just a week before she died. None of this is representative of a controlling relationship.

Brad often watched the girls while she was out with her friends. In fact, in the months prior to her death, she spent almost every evening out, and many times Brad was not even aware of where she was. He picked up Nancy and her friend Carey Clark one evening from a restaurant because they had been drinking and didn't feel comfortable driving home. He took the girls with him. Carey described him as "pleasant." Even the night before she went missing, Brad took the girls home while Nancy remained at the party.

It was unethical for prosecutors to misrepresent the state of the Coopers' marriage by depicting it as controlling. Chief Bazemore classified it as "domestic violence of the worst kind." Just after the trial, WRAL reported "Cooper case was about domestic violence." This was untrue. Nancy didn't contact Interact, she wanted Brad to share custody of the girls, she never told a single person she was afraid of Brad and the records and testimony from Nancy's longer term friends refuted all of the "controlling relationship" claims. Nancy's schedule the week leading up to her disappearance illustrates her level of freedom and also demonstrates her trust in Brad to care for the children because he would have watched them every evening that week.

Sunday, July 6, 2008: Nancy, Bella and Katie arrived home from Hilton Head, SC. They vacationed with her parents, Garry and Donna Rentz, her sister, Krista Lister, and her husband, Jim.

Monday, July 7, 2008: Nancy had a lot of phone activity all day. She spoke to Jessica Adam, Hannah Prichard, the children's pediatrician's office, the Sherwin Williams paint store, Nordstrom department store and the exterminator, Gary Beard.

- "Nancy cleaned the house all day." Source: Hannah

7:00-9:00p.m. – Nancy went to Jessica's house to set up for painting the next day. Source: Jessica's calendar, deposition

Tuesday, July 8, 2008:

9:45 a.m. – Nancy arrives at Jessica's to paint. Source: Jessica Adam's interview

10:30 a.m. – Garry Beard arrives at Cooper home. Nancy shows up after speaking to him on the phone. Girls at school. Source: Gary Beard's interview

5 – 7 p.m. – Brad came to Jessica's home, picked up the kids, Nancy stayed for another hour or two. Source: Jessica's deposition

7-9 p.m. – Nancy goes to Jennifer Fetterolf's home after painting at Jessica's. Source: Jennifer's interview

Wednesday, July 9, 2008:

Noon – Mary Anderson goes to Jessica's home and sees Nancy painting. Source: Jessica's deposition

1:00 – 3:30 p.m. – Mary Anderson, Jessica Adam and Nancy go to clothing boutique, Uniquities in Cameron Village, after picking the kids up from school. Nancy stated she had errands to run afterward. Nancy did not buy anything at Uniquities. Source: Mary Anderson's interviews

5:00 p.m. – Brad calls Nancy's cell, wants to see kids. Mary states Nancy, Brad and kids plan to go to Mike and Clea's home that night. Source: Mary Anderson interview

6:00 p.m. – Brad, Nancy and kids have dinner with Mike and Clea. Nancy leaves early because she is not feeling well. Source: Clea, Mike interviews

7:00 p.m. – Nancy leaves Mike and Clea's house and returns home. Nancy says she's not feeling well, but actually goes to Jessica's. Source: Jessica's interview

7 – 10:30 p.m. – Nancy goes to Jessica's house then returns home. Jessica thinks Nancy went to Jennifer Fetterolf's but Jennifer doesn't confirm. Source: Jessica's interview

Thursday, July 10, 2008:

10:30 a.m. – Nancy and Hannah run at Crossroads Apartment building gym. Source: Hannah

Nancy buys dress at Uniquities, unknown time. Source: Kinde interview

Nancy told Carey Clark she went running on Thursday at Lake Johnson Source: Carey Clark

Friday, July 11, 2008:

11:30 – 2 p.m. – Nancy, Hannah and Susan Crook at Hannah's community pool. Source: Hannah

2:54 p.m. – Nancy buys food for barbecue at Harris Teeter, picks up Katie's prescription. Source: Harris Teeter surveillance video

3:45 – 5:30 p.m. – Jessica at Cooper home Source: Jessica

Nancy makes phone calls from landline phone at 3:18 p.m. and again at 4:26 p.m. and 4:40 p.m.

6:30 p.m. – Nancy, Bella, and Katie go across the street to the Duncans' home.

8:15-8:30 p.m. – Nancy walks Brad and the girls home then returns to the party.

Midnight – Nancy leaves Duncans' party, returns home.

{ 10 }

The Custody Case

Things snowballed very quickly after the accusations were made against Brad in the 911 call. On July 16, 2008, just two days after Nancy's body was found, Nancy's parents Garry and Donna Rentz and her sister, Krista Lister, secretly filed for emergency custody of Bella and Katie Cooper. Their attorney Alice Stubbs along with Detective Jim Young had an ex parte meeting with Judge Sasser. The motion[39] for emergency custody cited erroneous claims that even if true, were not justifiable reasons for removing the children from Brad. An ex parte hearing consists of one party meeting with the judge. The judge only hears one side and the other party has no opportunity to refute the claims. The judge has the right to refuse to deny the motion or he/she has the opportunity to inform the other party and give them the opportunity to respond to the allegations included in the emergency motion, but Brad did not have an opportunity to respond. The motion was granted, and his girls were ripped from his arms.

The motion listed the following reasons for believing the children were in danger – Brad had had an affair (4 years prior), Brad attempted suicide in the past (not true), Nancy had to borrow money from family to buy food for the children (not true). It also described the fact that Nancy had been murdered and that her body was found by a third party. It further stated that the home was being investigated as a crime scene. Again, though police had suspicions about Brad, there was no evidence whatsoever that he had any involvement in Nancy's death. As well, the separation draft specified that the Coopers would share custody of the girls. There was never any indication that Nancy wanted to keep the girls away from their father. Removing the girls from Brad's care combined with the police chief's early statements unjustly cemented the community's suspicions about Brad, making it easier for the police to build their case against Brad. People had to think, "He must be guilty . . . why else would they remove the children from him?"

As Brad was trying to cope with the shocking news of Nancy's death, Garry and Donna Rentz contacted him two days after the body was found and requested to see the girls. They were to meet at Bullwinkle's, a children's play center. Brad was blindsided as he was met by police when he arrived. They were there to take the children from him. It was devastating for Brad and for the girls who cried all the way to the police station where the Rentzes were waiting for them. There could have been a gentler way to handle this, but that is what the Rentzes chose to do.

Brad described the painful exchange in an affidavit.

> "I never refused to allow the Plaintiffs to visit with the girls. In fact, I was bringing the girls to meet with them and visit with them at Bullwinkle's on July 16, 2008, when I was served with the ex parte order removing them from my custody. The Plaintiffs never came. They were strangers to the girls. Bella was

frightened and cried. I tried to calm Bella down and told them they would be going on a fun vacation, once I understood what was happening and the police explained to me what the Plaintiffs had done. Bella refused to let go of me. Her arms were wrapped around my neck and her legs around my waist. The police officers had to pry her from me while she screamed and cried. I tried not to show my own feelings while the girls were there because I did not want to upset them further. Bella and Katie would not have gone through that trauma if the Plaintiffs had simply come to get the girls themselves. We had already planned for them to visit with the girls. They could have handled it without causing a scene and I could have provided better for the girls needs and given them clothes, their favorite toys and their medicines."[40]

This is how one Wake county deputy described the incident. Many had similar reports.[41]

Now comes the undersigned affiant, Deputy Alvis Speight, being first duly sworn, and says the following:

1. My name is Deputy Alvis Speight. I am over eighteen years old, and I am competent to testify to the matters set forth herein.
2. I am a deputy with the Wake County Sheriff's Department.
3. I was one of the law enforcement officers that helped execute a court order to assign temporary custody of Isabella ("Bella") and Gabriella ("Katie") Cooper to their grandparents, Donna and Garry Rentz.
4. Bella is four years old and she started to cry and scream during the custody exchange. She wanted her daddy and was clinging on to him.

5. When we put the girls in the car they both acted like they were frightened. Bella was crying and holding onto her daddy. Katie also seemed concerned. Brad told the girls that there were going to see grandma in an effort to calm them down.

6. Bella cried for the entire ride from her dad to the police station. She kept asking for her daddy.

7. One of the little girls seemed to be scared of the male officers assisting in their removal.

8. Donna and Garry Rentz did not come with us to get the girls. Instead, they waited for the girls at the police station.

9. Brad was very cooperative throughout this ordeal.

Choosing Sides

At the time of the ex parte hearing, Nancy's friendship clique was encouraged to write affidavits of support for Nancy's family seeking permanent custody of the girls. People were under pressure to pick a side—either they were on the side of "Brad did it" and agreed to write an affidavit for Nancy's family, or they were excluded from the social circle. Jessica seemed to be the ring leader of that effort, and there was encouragement for friends to adopt her thoughts. She wanted the affidavits to include consistent statements

"So you know we have no idea who's doing what. You know, the whole taking sides thing. We don't know whose side to take." (Sharon Baughman – interview with Cary police 7/26/08)[42]

". . . They're asking people to choose sides too. I mean, I don't know how much of that you've seen in the affidavits, but they've literally had people on the phone crying because they didn't do an affidavit." (Mike Hiller, 7/30/08)[43]

The pressure within the friendship clique was intense. Jessica tried to persuade Carrie Dittner to write an affidavit for Nancy's family, and when she refused, she cut off ties with her.

"Jessica Adam talks with Carrie about filing affidavit on behalf of Nancy. Jessica gives Carrie ultimatum." (Detective Dismukes hand notes 8/8/08)

Diana Duncan threatened to sever ties with Clea if she didn't write a negative affidavit. Clea gave in to the pressure and wrote an affidavit with many of the same negative stories about Brad contained in other affidavits.

Diana Duncan's Depostion 10/6/08
Q. (By Ms. Sandlin , Brad's attorney) Do you see the portion that's highlighted?
A. Yes. What about it?
Q. Is that what you're speaking about?
A. Yes
Q. And what were the consequences if Clea were to still be in contact with Brad?
A. I was not going to have a relationship with her anymore.
Q. Have you said that to anyone else?
A. No.
Q. Why not?
A. No one else that I've talked to is still having a relationship with Brad that I'm aware of.

89

Q. Then you say, "We cannot tolerate anyone in our lives to have divided loyalties at this point." What does that mean?

A. That means in the state of fear that we're in, we can't, you know, talk to someone who I think is going to go behind my back and talk to Brad.

Q. About anything?

A. About anything.

Q. Or that supports Brad in any way?

A. Yeah. I mean, I support my friends and anyone's right to support Brad and to believe whatever they think, and I support his right to counsel. And I support his right to fairness. I'm very, very sure about that. But I don't need to talk to anyone who is talking to Brad.

Q. So you wouldn't have any relationship with anyone who was having anything to do with Brad?

A. Other than maybe light social – I can go to a kid's party with someone, sure.

Jessica Adam oddly described how associating with people who believed Brad was innocent would create legal challenges.

Jessica Adam Deposition 10/6/08

Q. Have you ever told anyone that they have to decide what their loyalties are –

A. No.

Q. If you'll let me finish.

A. Sure.

Q. Have you ever told anyone that they must decide their loyalty with regard to whether they're on Brad's side or on the side of the people who believe that Nancy was murdered?

A. No.

Q. Do you believe that?

A. Do I believe what?

Q. That people have to decide which side they're on?

A. No. People can do whatever they want to do, but I'm in charge of myself.

Q. Well, if someone sides with Brad, is that someone you're going to continue a friendship with?

A. Probably not, because it would get, I'm sure on a legal level challenging, and I don't need that right now.

Q. Why would it be challenging on a legal level?

A. Because I don't want to make any mistakes, you know, of any sort. This is a complicated scenario.

Q. What do you mean you wouldn't want to make any mistakes?

A. Meaning, I, you know I'm handling myself only. If someone wants to be filing documents on Brad's behalf, then best I steer clear.

Jessica, Hannah and Diana collaborated and held affidavit meetings, and in the end all of the affidavits for the Rentz family contained very similar and in some cases identical statements. Jessica shared hers with Jennifer Fetterolf.

"Hey, Jess, thanks for the statement. It will help me wrap my head around what I need to say and help remember a lot of stories, some in similarity, that Nancy and I used to share and talk about." (Email from Jennifer Fetterholf to Jessica Adam)[44]

Craig Duncan had initially agreed to write an affidavit for Brad, but after a visit from Jessica and Brett Adam, he was convinced not to write it. There was tremendous pressure for everyone to be against Brad. Why would the Adams care if Craig wrote an affidavit in support of Brad?

Diana Duncan deposition

Q. Do you recall that your husband, Craig had initially agreed to give an affidavit for Brad?

A. What I recall is that Craig agreed to meet with Brad's lawyers and then decided not to.

Q. Did Brett Adam come over to the house the night before Craig was supposed to come over and meet with the lawyers?

A. I don't remember. I remember Brett coming over, but I don't remember it in context.

Q. Prior to that night, how many times had Brett Adam come to your house alone?

A. I don't think I recall a time that he had come over.

Q. What was the purpose of his visit that night?

A. From what I remember, he just wanted to talk.

Q. He wanted to talk about Craig giving an affidavit, did he not?

A. Not that I recall, no. I don't remember talking about that.

After the visit from the Adams, Craig decided against writing the affidavit for Brad. The custody case had a huge influence on the over-all case because all of the stories included in the affidavits were relayed at the custody hearing and again at Brad's trial. No one had anything negative to say about Brad's parenting, so they attacked his character by referencing the affair. They portrayed him as a controlling husband because he put Nancy on a budget. He was attacked for training too much for an Ironman competition, for being an introvert, for working late and for attending an MBA program. He was accused of additional affairs that never happened and accused of disappearing for a weekend to attend a boat show and failing to call Nancy. He was accused of listening in on Nancy's phone calls via a Cisco phone and accused of disconnecting calls between Nancy and Jessica. None of it was true, and Brad's affidavit and those written by his family and friends refuted the accusations, but that didn't stop attorneys from eliciting statements from witnesses to first take his children from him and then to put him away for life.

Cary Police Formed Alliance with In-Laws' Attorneys

Cary Police worked very closely with the Rentzes' custody attorney, Alice Stubbs. It essentially created a dual prosecution as police worked in concert with the law firm and their investigators. Both had something to gain. The attorneys would win custody of the girls for Nancy's family, and this would leave an impression with the community that he must be guilty – making it that much easier to prosecute Brad for Nancy's murder. The law firm's investigators told witnesses not to speak to the defense, so few were willing to meet with Brad's defense team. The association should have given Brad's attorneys a right to receive all discovery materials related to the law firm's interactions and assistance to police with the investigation, but every motion for the discovery was denied.

Details of the relationship between police and law firm:
- Counsel for the in-laws disclosed to police information about the Coopers' finances.

- Counsel for the in-laws told police that she was suspicious of Brad's involvement in Nancy's death, supplying details apparently gleaned directly from Nancy.
- When witnesses asked police what they could do to assist with the investigation, the detectives replied, "Have you spoken to Alice Stubbs yet?", as if it were appropriate for witnesses in a homicide investigation to interview with family law attorneys embarking on a civil case against Brad.
- The law firm had its own investigators. The firm dissuaded witnesses from interviewing with defense investigators. Many witnesses complied and refused to speak to Brad's defense team.
- Police inserted themselves into the civil custody suit. Detective Daniels wrote an affidavit in support of the plaintiffs. Brad's attorneys filed a subpoena requesting discovery related to the origin of the detective's statements made in the affidavit. Judge Sasser denied the request.
- Officer Byrd and Detective Young of the Cary Police Department attended an ex parte motion in the custody matter, already taking sides, already assured of Brad's guilt.
- Cary police supplied Jessica Adam with phone records in preparation of her deposition with Brad's attorney.
- During the custody hearing, the in-laws' counsel played a version of the 911 tape obtained from police that had not been shared with Brad's attorneys, even though they had requested it.
- There is information in Discovery indicating the Cary Police supplied Nancy's family with a car.
- It appeared that police supplied the in-laws' counsel with a list of questions to ask Brad in his deposition.

"Gut Feelings"

Although this was a hearing to determine the best placement of the children, the in-laws' attorneys tried to suggest that there was reason to believe Brad was responsible for Nancy's death and therefore should lose his children. What evidence did they present? Nothing but speculation and gut feelings.

Hannah Prichard's testimony 10/16/08

Q. What is your fear about the children's safety?

A. I don't believe Brad Cooper is a stable person.

Q. Based on what?

A. Based on the fact that I believe he killed Nancy Cooper.

Q. And why do you believe that?

A. Because it's what makes sense to me, and it is my gut feeling.

Q. Well, other than your gut feeling, why do you believe that?

A. It's what makes sense to me.

Q. Any other reasons?

A. No.

The rest of the testimony was based on the unsubstantiated claims stated in the affidavits described above. Nothing suggested that Brad was unable to properly care for his children. Just weeks after the hearing, on October 27, 2008, Brad was indicted and charged with first degree murder. Days later, Judge Sasser ruled that the girls would remain in the temporary custody of Nancy's family. In April 2009, Brad's custody attorney Deborah Sandlin filed a motion requesting a postponement of the permanent custody hearing until after Brad's trial. It was denied. On May 15, 2009, Nancy's family was granted permanent custody of his two daughters.

{ 11 }

Botched Attorney-Client Privilege Agreement

The prosecution acted improperly by ignoring Brad's attorney-client privilege rights with regard to specific items in this case. Before delving into this, it's important to understand exactly what is subject to this privilege.

"One of the basic tenets of the relationship between an attorney and the client is that any information which passes between the two remains confidential. This concept is also known as the attorney-client privilege. Based on early English common law, the idea of privilege is a simple one—a client maintains the privilege to refuse to disclose or to have an attorney disclose any communications that occur while one is seeking legal advice.

"This privilege is important as it allows a client the comfort to disclose all necessary factual information to an attorney without fear that such discussions will harm the client's case. While an attorney may invoke the privilege on behalf of a client, the right originates with the client. The client and not the attorney decides which information is confidential and should remain privileged and advises the attorney accordingly." [45]

On July 16, 2008, police searched the Coopers' home and collected property items into evidence. This left Brad without a computer, so he purchased a new one. It enabled him to communicate electronically with his attorneys and family and to share documents and other items. Brad was arrested in October 2008, and at that point police confiscated his new computer. Brad's attorney, Howard Kurtz, made a request of Assistant District Attorney (ADA) Cummings to refrain from viewing the computer until a determination could be made about what information qualified as privileged material. He refused.

In November 2008, Brad's attorney formally notified the state that Brad's computer which was purchased after the search qualified as privileged material. This was discussed by both parties in court, and it was agreed that they would work together to find a way to protect the material. ADA Cummings recommended that Howard Kurtz contact the FBI to discuss the best way to protect the information. After Howard discussed it with Special Agent Johnson, they agreed that the best plan of action would be for a second FBI examiner to make a mirror image of the drive and give it to the defense. The agent would be someone not assigned to the investigation since it was privileged material. There was also an understanding that the State would not receive any protected digital media.

In May 2009, Detective Young of the Cary Police delivered one *of two copies* to Howard Kurtz. ADA Cummings explained that one copy was for the defense, the other for the State. ADA Cummings agreed not to examine it but provided no explanation for why a second copy had been made. In June 2009, Brad's attorney was forced to file a motion to compel the state to relinquish possession of privileged material.

Subsequently, Brad's attorney asked Agent Johnson why he refused to honor the agreement to make one copy, and at that point Agent Johnson told him that he did not even use an independent examiner – that he himself made the copies. He said that <u>ADA Cummings contacted him and told him to disregard everything that he and Brad's attorney had agreed on, to make two copies and to deliver them to Detective Young</u>. Mr. Cummings stated that he did not contact Agent Johnson, Cary Police did. This is impossible to verify at this point in time.

The State asserted that Brad Cooper waived his right to protection under attorney-client privilege and work product because he participated in a custody deposition. Judge Rand was appointed to oversee the conflict with the attorney-client privilege issues. In August 2010, Judge Rand concluded that 479 documents were protected under attorney-client privilege and work product. However, that wasn't the end of it. The state then claimed that Brad waived his rights to protection, so Judge Rand was requested to rule on that claim. In November 2010, just four months before trial, Judge Rand held that protections were *not* waived and that the State should not be permitted to view the material. After everything that occurred in the legal proceedings, Brad won this battle. However, they had the disc all along, and it is impossible to know if they honored the agreement. It is probably safe to bet that they did indeed examine all of the contents of the disc. There are no consequences to police and prosecutors for disregarding one's rights.

{ 12 }

Mishandled Evidence

Brad's computer was so severely mishandled that it should have been deemed inadmissible by the court, but Judge Gessner allowed the State to present the unreliable evidence. As each mistake by investigators is explored, remember that this was the only evidence used to convict him. One of the first issues was broken chain of custody. Police failed to follow proper chain of custody procedures in the handling, storage and documentation of Brad's IBM ThinkPad computer. It is crucial to follow and document proper chain of custody for all evidence but even more so with digital evidence because it so very susceptible to tampering.

> **Chain of custody**, in legal contexts, refers to the chronological documentation or paper trail, showing the seizure, custody, control, transfer, analysis, and disposition of physical or electronic *evidence*.
>
> When evidence can be used in court to convict persons of crimes, it must be handled in a scrupulously careful manner to

prevent tampering or contamination. The idea behind recording the chain of custody is to establish that the alleged evidence is in fact related to the alleged crime, rather than having, for example, been "planted" *fraudulently* to make someone appear guilty.[46]

To avoid confusion, here is a list of people who handled the computer evidence in this case.

Experts for the Prosecution:
Special Agent Gregory Johnson, FBI – Computer forensic examiner
Officer Chris Chappell – Durham Police Department – assigned to the FBI Cybercrime task force – Assisted SA Johnson

Experts for the Defense
Jay Ward – Network Security Expert – Several years experience identifying network vulnerabilities, skilled at identifying intrusions (or hacking) of computers
Giovanni Masucci – Senior Digital Forensic Examiner

Cary Police Detectives
Detective Young – involved in seizure and storage of electronic evidence, coordinated forensic examinations with FBI agents
Detective Ice – Collected and transported evidence from the Cooper home to police department
Detective Bonin – Initiated FBI involvement in the Nancy Cooper homicide investigation

Police seized evidence from the Cooper home on July 15, 2008. Brad's computer was left on and connected to the wireless network for twenty- seven hours, but there will be more about forensic protocol issues later. The next day they transported the computer along with other evidence to the police station but suspiciously chose not to secure this particular item in the Cary Police Department's evidence room. It is standard practice for evidence to be placed in the locked evidence room where a signature is always required to sign an item into evidence, to review the item or to transfer it to another agency.

In this particular case, they placed the computer in a lab. It is basically a room that is used for forensic examinations of electronic evidence. It is locked, but not secure. Three people hold a key to the room, but even if the door is locked, there is no signature required when evidence is removed or someone enters the room to examine evidence. One could easily enter the room, tamper with the evidence, and leave and none of the actions would be documented in any way. This is broken chain of custody.

Detective Young instructed Detective Ice to place the computer in the unsecure lab. Detective Ice described the general purpose of the lab. He said that the *normal* procedure would be to sign an item out of the evidence room when an investigator wishes to examine it and carry it over to the lab for any required forensic examinations. Once the examination is complete, the evidence would be signed back into the evidence room. Signatures would document the whereabouts of the evidence at all times. Police provided no explanation for the decision to place the computer in the unsecure lab instead of the evidence room. Cary Police arranged to have the FBI examine the computers in this case, so all of the computers should have been in the evidence room the entire time and never in the computer lab.

Chain of custody issues didn't stop there. Detective Bonin of the Cary Police Department was assigned to the FBI task force, and he initiated the FBI's involvement in the analysis of the computers in this case. Bonin was responsible for delivering the computers to the FBI office. According to Cary Police evidence sheets, there was a handoff from Detective Young to Detective Bonin on July 25, 2008. However, the FBI evidence sheet indicates that Detective Thomas handed the computer to Detective Bonin on July 28, 2008. That means that there are three days when the computer was officially signed over to Detective Bonin, but he did not have physical custody of the item. It could have been anywhere. Again, this is broken chain of custody.

Detective Young testified that he verbally informed Detective Bonin on July 25 that the computer was now signed over to him, but that it was still in the computer lab. Detective Thomas testified that he physically handed the computer to Detective Bonin on July 28. Why would there ever be two separate handoffs to the same person but on different dates? Surely police should have been aware of the importance of proper change of custody. It is very suspicious, but this would be one of many ignored protocols. We are simply to "trust" that nothing nefarious happened to the computer while it was in police custody. Protocols protect the evidence, and when they are ignored there can be no assurance that the evidence is reliable. While chain of custody and proper storage is important, proper collection of digital evidence is also critical in maintaining its reliability.

Forensic protocols ensure that digital evidence is properly handled and not subject to manipulation or tampering so that it can hold up in court. CISSP (Certified Information Systems Security Professional) is a standard in computer security and recognized and followed by many government agencies. It describes proper procedures that *must* be followed:

> Computer forensics and proper collection of evidence: Forensics is a science and an art that requires specialized techniques for the recovery, *authentication*, and analysis of electronic data for the purposes of a criminal act. Specific processes exist relating to reconstruction of computer usage, examination of residual data, and *authentication of data* by technical analysis or explanation of technical features of data, and computer usage.[47]

As mentioned, when police entered the home on July 15, they left Brad's computer on and connected to the wireless internet for 27 hours, leaving it exposed to intrusions and tampering. The computer was on a WEP (Wired Equivalent Privacy) system which is known to be insecure.[48]

> WEP was the first standardized way of securing wireless networks. It encrypts your data—which is good—but doesn't stop people from eavesdropping – which is bad. The main problem with WEP is that it's been solved, <u>meaning anyone can break into a WEP network using freely available tools.</u>

Police should have immediately unplugged Brad's computer, removed the contents of the RAM, and transported it to the Cary Police Department evidence room where further measures could have been taken to ensure the integrity of the evidence. One of the first things forensic examiners typically do after seizing computer evidence is make a copy of the hard drive and then run a hash. A hash value is an easy way to verify that data hasn't been altered so it needs to be done right away.

> Producing *hash values* for accessing *data* or for *security*. A hash value (or simply *hash*), also called a *message digest*, is a number generated from a *string* of text. The hash is substantially smaller than the text itself, and is generated by a formula in such a way that it is extremely unlikely that some other text will produce the same hash value.[49]

Hashing allows investigators to document that evidence hasn't changed while it's in their custody. If Cary Police had obtained a hash value, they could have supplied the value to the FBI so they could compare it to their own initial and post-analysis hash value. That would have proven that no files were modified, deleted or added before and after their analyses. The FBI also failed to run a hash until thirteen days after receiving the computer. At that point, it was a waste of time to run it at all because there is no way to verify that changes hadn't been made *after* police seized it. This was a huge forensic oversight that can't be ignored when considering the integrity of the evidence.

There are dozens of documents that stress the importance of preserving digital evidence and how failure to do so will deem the evidence inadmissible. However, a non-objective judge may accept unreliable evidence, despite clear evidence of broken chain of custody and tampering. Judge Gessner accepted the evidence even with all the issues described thus far, and it gets much, much worse.

Third-Party Verification

"The biggest challenge for the prosecutor is to 'put the Defendant's fingers on the keyboard.' In other words, the prosecutor must show that the computer crime, if any, was committed by the Defendant and not someone else on the same computer."

- Jeremy Rosenthal [50]

The FBI discovered the Google map files on Brad's computer on September 5, 2008. This would turn out to be the only evidence linking Brad to Nancy's death, but investigators never bothered to *verify* that Brad did the search. It was alleged that Brad did a Google map search of Fielding Drive at 1:14 p.m. on July 11, 2008—one day before Nancy disappeared.

This was yet another forensic protocol that was suspiciously ignored. It is standard practice for law enforcement to subpoena the service provider – in this case *Google* for these records. Cary Police subpoenaed Google for several records throughout the investigation, but never bothered to preserve the most important evidence in the case. In fact, just after FBI Agent Johnson discovered the Google map files, measures were taken to preserve one of Brad's email accounts at Google but not the map files.

9/15/08	6742	Maria Jocys (FBI)	FBI Letter to Google Save data on bbsimple account.

Detective Dismukes also sent a court order to Google on 9/16/08 and also failed to include the map files.

"Any and all records and other evidence, to include, but not limited to groups, search history, talk, 'Google' checkout, logs, log files and e-mails sent to and from this e-mail account for the peri-

107

od of time from the date the account was created/established to present. Any and all IP addresses from which this e-mail account was accessed to include but not limited to the IP address associated with the creation/establishment of the e-mail account."

Detective Young referenced the email account again in a search warrant dated 12/2/08. Again, *no mention of the map search*! Agent Johnson testified that he told Cary Police to subpoena Google to preserve the search files, but there is no documentation to prove that assertion and besides, why didn't he do it himself? He is the one who allegedly found the map files. He made sure the e-mail account was preserved, *why not the map files*?

Aside from verification through Google, investigators could have verified the search in other ways. They could have examined Brad's home routers, network logs and Cisco servers for a Google map search at that time. They did absolutely nothing to verify that the search originated on Brad's computer at 1:14 p.m. on Friday, July 11, 2008, thus no proof exists that Brad did the search. Is there a logical reason for them to overlook this aside from the obvious—that they would never be able to trace the IP address back to Brad because he didn't do the search?

Computer evidence has been important in many criminal cases and in every instance (except the Cooper case) investigators followed the proper procedure of third party verification, either through the search engine or the server. Here are a few examples to illustrate the point.

Ferrante case:
Following his wife's death, Robert Ferrante was accused of searching for "whether a machine at the hospital would be capable of removing

cyanide from a body." Police immediately applied for a search warrant for all identifying data regarding the Google internet query "would ecmo or dialysis remove traces of toxic poisons" generated on or about April 25, 2013, at 09:32:30 p.m. Data requested included date and time, whether the query was recorded by Google, the IP address from which any such query originated and any other identifying data derived from the query. [51]

McGuire case:

Melanie McGuire, age 33, used the Google search engine to find more ways to kill her husband, entering phrases like "undetectable poisons," "fatal digoxin levels," and "instant *poisons.*" Although some users might accuse Google for violating the users' privacy, the authorities ordered the company to provide the information while the search giant had nothing more to do than to agree with the demand and offer the information. [52]

Coleman case:

Computer evidence was important in the Coleman trial in May 2011, and again investigators confirmed the evidence with third party verification, "Ken Wojtowicz of the Granite City Police Department is a computer technician who testified Monday. There were a total of 7 emails sent from a destroychris@gmail.com account.
The tech says a subpoena sent to Google proves the gmail account and all 7 of the emails were linked to IP (internet protocol) addresses on Coleman's Dell laptop, provided by Joyce Meyer Ministries." [53]

Baker case:

The evidence, which eventually secured Mr. Baker's conviction, included data recovered from a laptop hard drive released by his church and the <u>main computer server</u> at a youth center where he also served. Computer forensic analysis was able to reveal that Mr. Baker had entered the term "overdose on sleeping pills" into a search engine and viewed several pharmaceutical websites prior to his wife's death[54].

In each of the above documented cases, investigators traced the activity to the suspects through third party verification sources. This is *standard* procedure for forensic examiners. It is the only way to prove that the computer activity was executed by the suspect, yet no explanation for neglecting to verify that Brad did the Google map search was ever provided. This indicates a lack of confidence in the reliability of the evidence and is a huge red flag.

Privacy Policies and Crucial Deadlines

Internet search providers have established privacy policies in place with restrictions on the length of time data is retained. It's unclear if Google still has the same policy in place now, but in 2008, Google removed all identifying data from *its half* of the cookie after 9 months. Time was very critical in this particular case. Brad's ability to prove his innocence depended on evidence being shared in a timely manner.

A cookie is a text file that's automatically saved to your computer every time you go to a web page. It stores information about your activity to make Internet browsing easier by keeping some of your preferences, like passwords and settings. If law enforcement finds a cookie on a computer, they can use a court order to make Google look up information about when, where, and by whom that search was done. It's a foolproof way to verify whether something digital (something that can easily be manipulated) is real. However, after nine months, the identifying information is scrubbed.

On October 9, 2008, Detective Daniels prepared an affidavit[55] for the plaintiffs who were seeking to take Brad's girls from him. He referenced the fact that the FBI was examining Brad's computers, as if the mere fact that they were being examined would somehow influence the judge about where to place the children. In light of this, Brad's attorneys filed a subpoena demanding immediate copies of the hard drives and all other discovery related to the investigation.

It is standard practice to first make a copy of the computer's hard drive to avoid potentially changing something on the original. It is not a complicated procedure, and it certainly wouldn't interfere with the examinations. ADA Howard Cummings was either ignorant about the process or he outright lied when he responded that the FBI couldn't make a copy until the examination was complete.

"It's also my information—and I am telling you what I know about certain things, but in any event, the examination of that computer is not complete. I asked if there were opportunity to reproduce the hard drive, and I am not a forensic computer expert. I barely know how to read my own emails, but it's my information that they did not make a copy of it and that they cannot make a copy until they get through with the examination, and that's what I was told." (ADA Howard Cummings – Custody hearing October 16, 2008)

The ADA blocked the defense from receiving evidence they were entitled to. The FBI received the computers on July 28, 2008, so they certainly should have made copies by the October 16 hearing. If not,

Brad's request for the copies should have been immediately granted, especially because time was so critical based on the privacy policies.

Despite filing several discovery motions, the defense wouldn't receive the images until May 2009—11 months after the FBI received the computers—which was two months after the privacy policy had *expired*. The FBI had actually finished their examination six months earlier, but defense motions for discovery were ignored until it was too late. They stalled until it would become impossible for *anyone* to verify (or disprove) that the search originated on Brad's computer. The opportunity was lost forever, and it seems obvious they intentionally delayed things to block Brad's ability to prove his innocence. Understand that since there was no DNA in this case, this digital evidence was Brad's only way to definitively prove that he was framed with the map files. The State destroyed that opportunity with no consequences for their egregious behavior.

{ 13 }

Statements Evolve to Fit Police Theory

Police had blinders on as they actively sought statements that supported their theory and ignored those that refuted it. Not only did they
seek specific statements, they coached and coerced witnesses to get
the information they needed to present their case to the District Attorney. Statements were actually created along the way as ideas emerged
to make Brad appear guilty. Police likely went this route because they
didn't have any evidence that pointed toward Brad's involvement in
Nancy's death. The corrupt nature of the investigation became clear as
information favorable to Brad was meticulously discarded.

As mentioned previously, the detectives worked very closely with
Jessica Adam and Hannah Prichard. They spoke frequently, emailed
each other and were on a first-name basis. Jessica and Hannah were
the two people who were strongly accusing Brad of harming Nancy,
and they were willing to do whatever was necessary to assist the police with their case against Brad, even if it meant lying. When police
needed a certain statement to support their theory, they went to them.

They had back-up support from the other clique members as well. It truly was a modern-day witch hunt.

Nancy's Running Plans

The morning of July 12, Brad told police that Nancy went for a run. This conflicted with Jessica's claim—that Nancy was expected at her house to paint. Both can't be right, so police needed to determine which was most likely—painting or running. Let's examine the statements and facts.

Nancy told *at least* three people at the Duncans' party that she planned to jog the next morning. Ricardo Lopez had a fairly lengthy discussion with Nancy. During his initial police interview he was matter-of fact about Nancy's plans to jog in the morning; however, he was somehow pressured to recant that statement.

Ricardo Lopez's interview with Detective Dismukes 8/20/08

Q. Did she mention anything about her plans for the following day?

A. Yeah, she said she was gonna go jogging. I could barely wake up, you know, that early to go jogging. It was kind of late. We didn't get back home 'til midnight so I was just thinking that . . . I mean that's all . . . that's what she said she was doing the next day.

Q. Nancy mentioned that she was going jogging?

A. She mentioned she was going jogging and I asked her, "Why . . . why are you going jogging?" You know, like . . . I don't know. Like

114

jogging to me is really not that great an exercise but she said she was preparing for a marathon so I'm like, "Oh well that makes sense."

Q. Was that towards the end of the evening or was that kind of . .

A. It was towards kind of halfway throughout.

Q. Did she say where she was going to go jogging at?

A. No.

Q. So she . . . .did she say what time or anything, what time she may be getting up?

A. Um, she said . . . it was . . . like first thing in the morning 'cause I remember thinking that – you know, the first thing I do is go down to get coffee and then try to find out what the kids are doing and uh, once I started to go running and I mentioned the only thing that I do is I take the dog for a walk but that's like 5 blocks. And you know, and then we talked about, you know, how much she runs and it's not just like around the block. She goes jogging for a while.

Later in the interview, Detective Dismukes informed Ricardo that he would be getting in touch with Ricardo's wife, Donna to clarify some things.

A. No. Just whatever you need, just let us know whatever we can do.

Q. Absolutely and I'll call definitely but I may be getting back in contact with Donna again because uh . . . just to get up with her to get some information . . . get some *clarifying* information, but I'll call her if I need to.

Two days later

Ricardo Lopez interview with Detective Dismukes 8/22/08

Q. Okay Mr. Lopez, uh you . . . uh, you called me yesterday, uh just in reference to uh, wanted to kind of update your story or update what you originally told me from your interview the other day.

A. Sure.

Q. Can you just go back and just refresh what you told me?

A. So what I originally told you that, uh, Nancy Cooper had said that she was going jogging the next morning, um, I got home and I started talking to my wife (Donna), and she mentioned that I had never told her that, especially the first couple of days after we heard . . .

Q. Um hmm

A. And um, so I started thinking further about it, and I think that's a pretty critical component—I don't know—in the case, so I didn't want to jeopardize anything and start thinking about it through. Um, and I don't think she ever actually said she was going jogging the next morning. I think that that's actually something I filled in, in my head. What I . . . what she did say is that she was a jogger and that she jogs and since I really don't like to jog or ever do jog, I just envisioned myself having to get up the next morning and it's like I just automatically thought that she said that to me. But there's no way that I would ever be sure that she said that. In fact, I just as soon say she didn't tell me that she was going jogging the next morning.

Lopez didn't want to *jeopardize* the investigation. Where did he get the impression that a statement about Nancy's jogging plans would jeopardize the investigation? There was clearly some type of coercion going on here, whether from police or the "friends." Police were probably unsettled about receiving a statement that Nancy had plans to jog the next morning. It was late August already, six weeks into the investigation. They were already deeply entrenched in their belief that Brad killed Nancy. They were only interested in information that supported their theory, and when they received contrary information, they managed to make it go away.

Police manipulated a second witness to support the painting story. Ross Tabachow told Detective Daniels on July 12, 2008 that Nancy had plans to *exercise* on Saturday morning. The statement was recorded in Daniels' hand notes.[56]
Tabachow subsequently interviewed with Detective Dismukes on July 28, 2008 and was coached to provide a statement that he overheard Nancy confirm painting plans for Saturday morning.

Ross Tabachow interview with Detective Dismukes[57]

Q. Well, let me go back to uh . . . so you heard her talking to Jessica Adam when Jessica called?

A. Um hmm.

Q. And what did you hear her say? Did she . . . <u>did you hear her, uh, say a specific time when she was going to be there</u>?

A. <u>No. No. I didn't hear any specific times</u>. I just heard some more painting.

Q. Okay.

A. And you know . . . I didn't even hear anything specifically about Saturday or Sunday or anything like that. It sounded like during the weekend. And I will say I know it wasn't Sunday night because later on in the evening, more or less after . . . I think it was after everybody except the five of us . . . and our kids were at the party. Um, I was telling everybody I had just gone on a camping trip with my brothers and caught . . . we caught some big fish and we've got this big . . . big fillet and you know ,"Why don't we have the Duncans and Nancy and the kids over to my house on Sunday night for dinner."

Q. <u>So she had . . . she had mentioned to you about going over to Jessica's Saturday morning?</u>

A. Well, I mean, on Saturday.

Q. <u>Okay, on Saturday.</u>

A. On Saturday at some point in time.

Note how his statement from his first interview – Nancy having "exercise plans" for Saturday was altered during his second interview. Now there was no mention of exercise plans. That statement was completely discarded and replaced with him having overheard confirmation of painting plans for "some time that weekend" and then with coaching it evolved to "painting plans for Saturday." Cary Police prepared a PowerPoint to go even one step further to include a specific time on Saturday that Tabachow never stated in his interview. The level of manipulation is alarming as this demonstrates that police actually *molded* the witness statements to match their theory.

"Interview with Ross Tabachow about party on July 11: Ross over-hears Nancy's phone call with Jessica Adam. He hears Nancy and Jessica agree about painting somewhere around *9 or 10 a.m.* on Saturday."

Painting Plans?

Obviously police refused to acknowledge Nancy's plans to jog on Saturday morning, but were there facts supporting Jessica's claim – that Nancy planned to paint? Police already knew there was a conflict for later that morning, because Nancy had agreed to watch the children while Brad played tennis. The tennis match was set for 9:30 a.m., and the plans were verified by police, so there was no room for doubt.

> "Mike told me Friday night (July 11) after he made plans with Brad to play tennis for Saturday morning, he went to Nancy and told her that he and Brad were going to play tennis tomorrow. According to Mike, he asked Nancy if it was OK for Brad to play tennis. Mike said he told Nancy that he and Brad were going to play at 9:30 a.m." (Detective Dismukes narrative #131, 7/30/08)[58]

What about Jessica's schedule that morning? There was no mention of painting plans on her calendar. She had other obligations written on the calendar for that morning though. Her two-year-old daughter had a swim lesson at 10:30, and her four-year-old son had a soccer game at 11:00. Is it realistic that she would have tried to squeeze in painting that morning too? Furniture would need to be moved; taping would need to be done. No additional paint had been purchased. It seems unlikely.

It is also odd that Jessica didn't take either child to their respective activities. She told police that she went to the gym with Mary Anderson and that she arranged for Mary's husband, Kip to take their son to soccer while her husband, Brett, took their two-year-old daughter to her swim lesson. There is no evidence that police ever attempted to verify any of that information, even though a conflict existed in the timeline. Nancy had *confirmed* plans to watch the children. The Adams could have been anywhere that morning.

Jessica's claim that Nancy was expected at her house to paint was not corroborated by a single person in initial interviews, but statements evolved over time. Several people were questioned on July 12 when Nancy was still a missing person. No one reported anything about Nancy's plans to paint at Jessica's, but witnesses (in addition to Ross Tabachow) included that detail in later interviews. Wouldn't it have been important to tell police the day she disappeared, "Oh, I know for sure that Nancy made plans to paint at Jessica's?" No one made any such statement. Carey Clark told police only that she and Nancy didn't have plans to run that morning, but in a later interview she added a statement about painting plans.

7/12/08: Told police that she and Nancy did not have plans to run on Saturday. Nothing more was added (Carey Clark, police report).[59]

↓

8/2/08: "No plans to run on Saturday. Nancy told Carey that she was <u>supposed to help a friend paint</u> on Saturday morning." (Carey Clark, Detective Dismukes hand notes)[60]

Carey's statement didn't work, because she claimed that Nancy informed her of her plans to paint on Friday at 5:20 a.m., but according to Jessica, the *plans were not even made* until Friday afternoon.

Hannah Prichard didn't mention anything about Nancy having painting plans during three initial interviews – on July 12, 15 and 22, yet during her deposition in October, she all of a sudden added that Nancy planned to paint on Saturday. That statement was also repeated at trial.

Hannah Prichard's deposition 10/9/08
Q. What were your plans for the next day?
A. She told me <u>she was going to try to get the painting done</u> at Jessica's house and then we were going to go to the pool.
(10/9/08 deposition)

Hannah's "new" statement didn't work because instead of calling Nancy's cell phone that morning, she called the Coopers' home phone, believing Nancy would be at home – not at Jessica's house. Diana Duncan did the same as the others. She didn't mention any knowledge of painting plans during her initial interview but added it in later interviews. So there were at least four people who were coerced to change their statements to *include* knowledge of Nancy's painting plans and at least two were coerced to *eliminate* the statement that Nancy had plans to jog or exercise.

Phone Call Versus "In Person" Plans
On July 12, Jessica told police that she and Nancy discussed and scheduled the Saturday painting plans *by phone* the prior day at 5:00 p.m. She stated this again in a second interview on July 15. When po-

lice obtained phone records and did not see that call, they questioned her about it, and at that point she *changed her story* to, "I was at the Coopers' home on Friday when the plans were made *in person*." This is yet more strong evidence that there were no painting plans. This witness flat out lied to police, but they weren't concerned with the changed story. At trial, Detective Dismukes testified that Jessica simply "clarified" things. She gave police false information, which makes all of her testimony questionable.

> "At this point in the interview, Detective Young and I asked Jessica to tell us her last contact with Nancy before she was reported missing. Jessica told us she talked with Nancy via <u>telephone around 5:00 p.m.</u> on Friday, July 11. (Detective Dismukes narrative #107 7/15/08)

The story changed on July 22.

> "<u>Jessica at Nancy's home around 4:30 p.m. on 7/11</u>. When Jessica arrived, Nancy not home, but at store. Jessica called Nancy and Nancy told Jess that she was on her way back." (Detective Dismukes – narrative #118, 7/22/08)

There was *no* call from Jessica's cell phone to Nancy's cell phone. There was a one-minute call at 3:05 p.m. from Jessica's *home phone* to Nancy's cell phone. Police had no problem with the lies, as long as they supported their theory. Its unlikely Jessica was actually at the Coopers' home on Friday. In fact, she placed five separate calls on her cell phone between 4:00 and 4:45 p.m. at a time when she alleged she was walking around the Cooper home with Nancy to discuss ways to organize the house. [61]

The time required to do the work
Jessica told Detective Dismukes that the painting would be a very detailed job and would take a lot of time.

> "Nancy told Jessica that the painting would probably take a couple of days and asked if that would be OK. Jessica told Nancy that was fine." (Detective Dismukes)[62]

. . . She told the prosecutor that it was to be a quick job.

> "She told us that the paint job Nancy was to do on the 12th was not a big job. She estimated that it would take 1.5 - 2 hours but Nancy could have thought it would have taken her only an hour. (Prosecutor Amy Fitzhugh 2/2/11)[63]

Nancy Running with Carey

Brad told police he *assumed* Nancy had gone running with Carey. The assumption was logical because Nancy had plans to run with Carey the prior day but cancelled. The two of them were training for a half marathon so often ran together. Again, statements changed to fit the police theory. Hannah Prichard's statement changed drastically.

1. "Brad said Nancy's not home." (initial interview)

2. "He *thinks* she went running with Carey."(subsequent interview)

3. "She *went* running with Carey." (Police presentation to DA. Statement attributed to Hannah)

Shouldn't the statement from the initial interview have carried the most weight? Police documented her statement to indicate that he simply said Nancy was not at home. By the time police met with the district attorney the statement had evolved to "She went running with Carey." At this point, police knew Nancy didn't go running with Carey so they wanted to make it appear as if Brad was 100% affirmative that Nancy went running with Carey to make it appear that he had lied. The twisting of witness statements was deceitful. Notice how each set of statements evolves over time until they ultimately take on a completely different meaning.

Statements attributed to Brad
7/12/08 "He *assumed* she went running with Carey."
10/27/08 "He thought she. . . ." (Cary Police PowerPoint)

Statements attributed to Hannah
7/12/08 "Brad said Nancy's not home."
7/15/08 "Brad did not indicate Nancy was running with anyone." (Dismukes handnotes)
7/22/08 "He thinks she went running with Carey." (audio)
7/22/08 "Run with Carey" (police narrative 120)
8/24/08 "He thought Nancy went running with Carey" (Dismukes hand notes)
8/24/08 "Nancy went running with Carey." (Dismukes supplemental)
10/9/08 "She had gone for a run with Carey, he believed." (deposition)

10/27/08 "She went running with Carey." (Cary Police PowerPoint)

Statements atrributed to Jessica

7/12/08 911 call – "Brad believed she went running with Carey."
7/15/08 "He knew Nancy was out and running with Carey." (Dismukes hand notes)
7/15/08 "With Carey. Matter-of-factly, as if he knew where she was." (Cary police narrative #107)
7/22/08 "Running with Carey" (Dismukes hand notes)
7/22/08 "Without hesitation, 'Nancy out for a run with Carey.'" (narrative # 118)
10-06/08 "Out for a run with Carey" (Deposition)
10-27-08 "She went running with Carey." (Cary Police PowerPoint)

3/12/10 – Cary Police PowerPoint "Brad advised running with Carey." (attributed to Hannah)

This type of thing happened over and over with so many witness statements. It shows how Cary Police were so desperate to show any semblance of evidence pointing toward Brad, but it just wasn't there so they had to twist things.

"Nancy running with her cell phone and keys"

Police tried to attach suspicion to the fact that Nancy left the home that morning without her keys and cell phone, even though there is no evidence that she would have typically carried those items with her while running. She would have had no need to take the keys because the Coopers had a garage keypad to gain access to the house. However, a story was concocted. Police asked Nancy's father, Garry Rentz, if Nancy normally took anything with her when she went running. Keep in mind that at this time, Nancy would see her parents about twice a year and had been living in North Carolina for the past eight years, but police decided to ask *them* about her typical routines.

"Daniels asked Garry if Nancy normally took anything with her when she went running. He stated Nancy would have <u>definitely taken her car keys with her</u> when she went running. He told us he taught his daughters to always run with their keys and to <u>keep one of the keys sticking out between their fingers so they could use it as a weapon</u> if they needed to." (Detective Dismukes, 7/14/08)[64]

Hannah Prichard backed up the "keys in a defensive position" statement.

"When asked if Nancy would run with anything in her hands, Hannah told us Nancy would have never left without her car keys for two reasons. One, to keep Brad from going through her car, and two, to <u>run with the keys between her fingers</u>." (Detective Dismukes 7/15/08)[65]

Carey was Nancy's running partner, yet she never noticed Nancy running with her keys in a defensive manner.

"Um, she would normally carry 'em in her hand or put 'em in her shorts. I've never seen her hold 'em like . . . <u>he asked me if she held 'em in a defense like</u> . . . like this, and <u>I've never seen her do that</u>." (Carey Clark, 8/2/08) [66]

Note that it would only make sense for Nancy to run with her keys if she drove to a location to run. Brad described the reason Nancy wouldn't have taken her keys with her while running from home during his deposition.

"She normally did not take her keys. <u>We have got a little keypad outside the garage door</u> that she – either one of us can enter the house using that so we wouldn't normally take a key."

Scott Heider also ran with Nancy.

"<u>It was not Nancy's habit to take her keys or cell phone with her on her runs.</u>" (Scott Heider affidavit 7/24/08)

Cary Police presented the DA's office with statements which were favorable to their case, such as "Nancy would run with her keys in a defensive position", and withheld information that was detrimental to their case, such as "Coopers' had a garage keypad to enter the house so Nancy wouldn't need to carry her keys.", even though the latter was an easily proven fact. They did this with numerous statements.

Cary Police PowerPoint
"Nancy used the vehicle and house key for protection when she ran alone which did not match with the keys being found in Brad's possession on July 12th."

Note: There is reason to believe the information contained in the PowerPoint was presented to the Grand Jury, though it is impossible to know exactly what was presented.

Necklace

Brad had to submit to a deposition as part of the custody case. If he refused, he would have to allow Nancy's family to maintain custody of his girls. Submitting to a deposition is a difficult decision when one is being investigated for a crime because it is actually a lengthy interrogation. In this case, police supplied the civil attorneys with questions for the proceeding. Criminal attorneys typically recommend that their clients don't respond to the civil suit because police can take any minor statement and claim the person is lying or being deceptive in some way, but Brad was willing to take that risk because he desperately wanted his children back. Immediately afterward, the media put the recorded deposition on their website for public viewing. It contained many intimate and personal details about Brad's private life, from specific information about past relationships to what type of allergy shots he received.

Naturally police viewed the deposition right away. All of a sudden several witnesses began stating that Nancy *never* removed her diamond pendant necklace. Brad had purchased it for Nancy in the fall of 2007.

Cooper Deposition 10/2/08

Q. What other items have you indulged her on?

A. I think October of last year, maybe November of last year she wanted a diamond necklace.

Q. November of 2007?

A. November or October of 2007, yes.

Q. And did she ask you for that?

A. Yes, she said that she had a bad year, and that she deserved it.

Q. And what was your response?

A. I said, "Well, let's go have a look at it and see if we can afford it."

Q. And what happened?

A. And, she had two picked out. One that was, I believe $7000, and one that was $2800.

Q. Where were those necklaces?

A. I believe the store was Bailey's.

Q. In Raleigh?

A. I believe so, yes.

Q. Did she purchase one of the necklaces?

A. I explained that we couldn't afford $7000 at that time, but we did purchase the one for $2800.

Q. Where is that necklace now?

A. <u>That one is currently in the residence.</u>

Q. Is that a necklace she wore frequently?

A. Yeah, I'd say she wore it fairly frequently, yes.

Q. Did she take it off?

A. <u>She did take it off, yes.</u>

(Underlined sections are emphasized by the author to highlight the main point of the questioning)

Prior to Brad's deposition, the necklace was mentioned in passing, but no one made the claim that she *never took it off*. They did not consider it noteworthy until they learned it was in the house.

"Diamond pendant *frequently* worn by Nancy." (Donna Rentz, 8/15/08)[67]

"Nancy had a necklace w/pendant (a bean) from Tiffany's – Jill has it now after getting same from house when in town for funeral." (Garry Rentz 8/14/08[68])

"I asked for her Tiffany Bean, her Lloyds of London pendant, and her other necklace that she had just purchased but my mom had given her. It was like a little butterfly that Nance had actually given that to Bella." (Krista Lister's deposition)

So, Nancy's mother mentioned that she frequently wore the diamond pendant, but her father and sister referenced other jewelry and did not mention the diamond pendant at all. On October 18, just a couple of weeks after Brad's deposition, Detective Daniels told Detective Dismukes to question Nancy's friends specifically about the diamond pendant necklace—and by friends that means the "go to" friends —Jessica and Hannah. They stated that Nancy *never* removed the necklace. Nancy's friend, Michelle Simmons made the same claim.

"Nancy purchased the necklace and <u>never took it off</u>." (Hannah Prichard, 10/18/08)[69]

"Dating back to when Nancy was first given the necklace (Oct. 07) through July 08, when she died, there were <u>absolutely no times that I saw Nancy without it on</u>." (Jessica Adam, written statement 10/21/08)[70]

"Michelle told me from what she knew Nancy always wore the necklace and <u>never took it off</u>. Michelle provided me with a <u>written statement on Nancy always wearing the necklace</u>. This written statement will remain on file with this case report." (Detective Dismukes supplemental report)[71]

At one point Hannah sent an email to Jennifer Fetterolf and copied Detective Dismukes. She specifically requested photos of Nancy wearing the necklace. She didn't ask for *all* photos of Nancy. Police wanted to be able to say, "Every photo received shows Nancy wearing the necklace." This shows that police conspired with witnesses to gain the statements they needed. Cary police could then use the "always wore necklace" claim as evidence of guilt.

Cary Police PowerPoint
"The other thing noted was that he never brought up the <u>necklace she wore all the time</u>. Also, the necklace was not on her, but was later learned that he had the necklace in his possession."

Police asserted that since Nancy *never* removed her necklace, that the killer must have removed it, and since the necklace was in the home, Brad must be the killer. There was a lot of trial testimony with witnesses repeating the same thing—"Nancy *never* removed her necklace." Like so many other things, it was false.

**Nancy Cooper Leaving Harris Teeter
July 11, 2008**

Cary police obtained the surveillance video of Nancy shopping at the Harris Teeter store on Friday, July 11. She would have been on her way home after having spent the afternoon at the pool with Hannah. Hannah testified that she was positive Nancy was wearing the neck-lace that day, yet Nancy was *not* wearing the necklace in the surveillance video. Hannah lied, and police completely ignored the video. Had the defense not reviewed the video and presented it during their case, we would have never seen it. This proves that police were aware that their claim about the necklace was false, but they used it anyhow to bolster their case. Further, they used witnesses to gather only photos with Nancy wearing the necklace in an attempt to prove their point. This was dishonest. The false claim became a big part of the State's case at trial. ADA Howard Cummings stated during clos-ing arguments that the surveillance images were "too grainy" to identify whether or not she was wearing the pendant. The prosecution tried to nail Brad with this, but they were 100% wrong. As well, Hannah Prichard was dishonest, and as a result, none of her testimony can be trusted.

Nancy's Earrings

When Nancy's body was found, she was wearing one diamond pendant earring. The other fell out due to decomposition. This presented another opportunity to bolster the State's case. Hannah updated her affidavit before Brad's trial stating that the earrings were "screwback," implying that the killer took the necklace but left the earrings because removing them would be too time-consuming. The truth is that the earrings had normal posts. The defense refuted her claim at trial, and she had to admit she was wrong about the earrings and had amended her affidavit with false information.

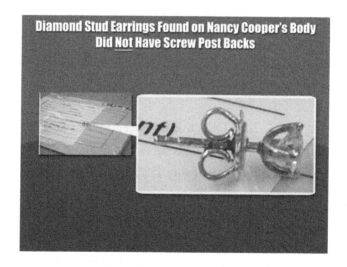

Diamond Stud Earrings Found on Nancy Cooper's Body Did **Not** Have Screw Post Backs

Nancy's Purse

Hannah's statements about Nancy's purse evolved over time and police appeared to instigate it. It was well documented that Nancy's purse was in her car the day she disappeared.

Initial Statements:

"Brad provided us w/pocketbook of Nancy Cooper from front rt. passenger seat." (Detective Young's hand notes 7/14/08) [72]

"Jessica stated she had her friend, Mary Anderson, drove her over to Nancy's house around 1:45 p.m. Jessica told us as soon as she arrived she went straight over to Nancy's car to see if her purse was inside. Jessica stated she saw Nancy's purse lying on the passenger side of the car." (Detective Dismukes)[73]

"Daniels asked Hannah if there was anything else we should know about Nancy and Brad Cooper. She told us Nancy always locked her purse inside her car with the car keys hidden." (Detective Dismukes, 7/15/08) [74]

On September 6, 2008 Detective Daniels told Detective Dismukes to ask Hannah *again* if Brad mentioned anything about Nancy's purse when they spoke the morning of July 12. This time she told police that Brad had Nancy's purse.

"At 1345 hours I spoke with Hannah Mathers (Prichard) via telephone. I asked Hannah if she recalled Brad saying anything about Nancy's purse or cell phone on Saturday, July 12. Hannah asked Brad where Nancy's purse and cell phone were. Brad told Hannah he had Nancy's purse and cell phone in front of him." [75]

This was another lie that appeared to be prompted by police. Hannah didn't voluntarily supply them with this information. Her original statement made no mention of Brad having the purse with him in the house that day. Surely she would have told them immediately if that were the case. The detectives sought that statement and she supplied it. They did this knowing that their own officers saw the purse in the car, not in the house!

Brad and Nancy "Looking at House on Fielding Drive"

On July 22, detectives asked Hannah if the Coopers ever looked at houses near the location where the body was found. She responded that she wouldn't have been surprised.

Hannah Prichard interview with Detective Daniels 7/22/08

Q. Um, did you ever know . . . did she ever tell you where they were looking for houses? Did she give you like, "We looked over here," or, "We looked over there"?

A. Oh yeah, they were looking . . . they were looking . . . you know, they were looking in my neighborhood in (inaudible) Park. Um, you know, I think she looked everywhere. Tom Garrett I'm sure could be more help with you with that.

Q. Okay.

A. But yes, she was looking everywhere and she wouldn't really tell me when she was looking on the other side of Cary because she knew I wanted her to stay over here.

Q. Okay, so you wouldn't have known if she was looking in the county or anything like that, or those houses off of Holly Springs subdivision?

A. It wouldn't surprise me if she was.

Q. Okay, but it . . . that would have been up until January?

A. Right, when she decided . . .

Q. In January, that was it. She didn't . . .

A. Right. That's right. [76]

Then, the detectives spoke with the Coopers' real estate agent, Tom Garrett, to see if they ever looked at houses on Fielding Drive. Nope.

Tom Garrett interview with Detective Dismukes 9/4/08

A. And, it's still November (talking about email paperwork that's going through). Good gracious, there was quite a spell of activities there. *When I talked to the other detective,* he also asked me had I ever shown them houses in the area where they found her body.

Q. Right.

A. That Toll Brother neighborhood, the price point was higher than what they were looking for. Since the base price in that neighborhood was high we never did go in there at all.

Q. Okay, Well, was uh, did Brad and Nancy . . . were they aware of the subdivision? I mean had they . . . had they said they looked back there before and asked you about it or did they just . . .

A. No . . . I . . . I just . . . I just never even . . .

136

Note: Detective Daniels pre-interviewed Tom Garrett about this same subject. He did not record any notes. He would often pre-screen witnesses and then send one of the other detectives to get a recorded interview. The pre-screen probably gave them an idea of questions to avoid. This way they already knew what the answers would be.[77]

Hannah's statement changed when Daniels told Dismukes to interview her a *second time* about the Coopers searching for homes near Fielding Drive.

> "At 1730 hours I contacted Hannah Mathers, per the request of Detective Daniels, to follow up with her about Nancy possibly purchasing a house. Hannah told me she was *sure* Nancy was looking at purchasing a house off Holly Springs Road near Fielding Drive. Hannah informed me she never went out with Nancy to look at houses but stated Nancy was looking in the Jamison Park subdivision and the <u>Holly Springs Road corridor</u>." (Detective Dismukes 9/8/08)[78]

So the statement went from "I wouldn't be surprised" to 100% affirmative that they looked in the Fielding Drive area. Police sought this statement even though the real estate agent told them that it was out of their price range and they never looked in that neighborhood. Weeks later, Hannah "remembers" more details.

> "Late fall of last year, on a Sunday, Brad and Nancy were driving around looking at houses. Hannah said Brad and Nancy were not with a realtor. She stated Nancy described the area they looked at was off Holly Springs Road close to Cary Parkway. <u>Hannah said she believes the neighborhood Brad and</u>

Nancy looked at was off Fielding Drive in the Oaks at Meadow Ridge." (Detective Dismukes 9/20/08)[79]

The detectives' two star witnesses never let them down. Both Jessica and Hannah were dishonest about so many things, yet police continued seeking their input; while ignoring obvious factual information.

Brad Calling Hannah for Information

During a July 22 interview, Hannah told Detective Dismukes that Brad called her twice on July 13. The content of the discussion evolved.

Detective Dismukes interview with Hannah Prichard 7/22/08
Q. We were talking about um Sunday night, Brad called you twice.
A. Yes.
Q. To ask if you had heard anything.
A. Right.
Q. I assume about the investigation . . .
A. The *search*.
Q. . . . . Or whatever. So, okay. Did he contact you? Is that pretty much what he wanted . . . the gist of that was he wanted to know if you'd heard anything?
A. Yes.
Q. Um hmm.

After the interview, Dismukes wrote a narrative and twisted Hannah's statement to inflect a completely different meaning.

"After Brad took Bella and Katie and returned home, Hannah stated she received two phone calls that evening from Brad asking if she had heard anything. She stated Brad asked her if there was *anything going on with the police*. Hannah stated she thought this was odd because there was a police officer stationed right outside of his house. She told us Brad said the police were asking him the same things over and over, and it was beginning to piss him off."
(Dismukes narrative #120 7/22/08)[80]

Hannah contacted Detective Dismukes one month later and repeated the story, but this time *she* added the information about Brad wanting her to contact the police for an update on the investigation and altered it further by also including Captain Williams' name.

"At 1400 hours I received a phone call from Hanna Mathers. Hannah stated she wanted to tell me about a conversation she had with Brad over the phone. Hannah said she received a call from Brad's home phone on July 13. According to Hannah, Brad asked her if she had heard anything. Hannah stated Brad asked her if she would call Captain Williams and ask what the status of the investigation is. Hannah said this request struck her as odd seeing that there was a Cary Police patrol car right outside Brad's house." (Detective Dismukes - supplemental report 8/22/08)[81]

What started with "Brad wanted an update on the *search*" evolved into Brad wanted the police captain contacted to find out about the

139

investigation. Hannah's trial testimony contained the evolved statement.

Hannah's Trial Testimony

Q. Did you have occasion to have a phone conversation with him later that day or night about the police and their questioning of him?

A. Yes. He had called at some point and <u>asked me if I had heard anything and suggested that I call Captain Williams</u>. I told him, wasn't there an officer outside his house? Why didn't he go ask him?

Q. What did you think about that question to you?

A. I thought it was strange.

Q. Why did you think it was strange?

A. If anybody could get information fast, it would be him.

Nancy's so called "loyal" friends were liars, and police encouraged it. This was perjury and police misconduct. Chief Bazemore had interesting notations in her handwritten notes about Nancy's friends.

- "Friends – private face to face"
- "Prejudicial issues"
- "Need for security"
- "Appreciative of them"
  (7/23/08 Bazemore notes) [82]

So there were multiple incidents where witness statements changed to support the police theory. This is proof of a dishonest investigation and it should have called the entire investigation into question but no one intervened and the deceptiveness continued in the same fashion, even into the trial. The prosecution supported the detectives' dishonest tactics.

{ 14 }

Alternate Suspects Never Considered

Police fully admitted that Brad Cooper was the only suspect from the beginning and throughout the investigation. They failed to explore the possibility of any alternate suspects. They overlooked Nancy's romantic entanglements, including a past affair with possible paternity implications and neighborhood men expressing interest in her shortly before her death. There were also unstable friendships and suspicious van sightings.

Nancy had a one-night stand with John Pearson on October 29, 2005, after a neighborhood Halloween party. At the time John was married to Kinde but later separated and divorced when his affair with Heather Metour became public. After the separation John moved out of the neighborhood and had little contact with neighbors after that time. Nancy's interactions with Pearson are relevant to the case for a few reasons. First, the two were in frequent contact with each other shortly before her death, second there is a possible paternity question regarding the Coopers' younger daughter, and third, Pearson withheld information from police and dramatically changed his story between interviews.

Pearson was initially interviewed on August 1, 2008. When asked about his activities during the time of Nancy's disappearance, he told police that he spent the night at Heather Metour's apartment July 11 and that he left at approximately 6:30 a.m. and went to pick up his children at his ex-wife Kinde Rawlin's house. He further stated that he spent the rest of the day with his children at home. Heather also told police that he spent the night at her place and left that morning to pick up the kids.

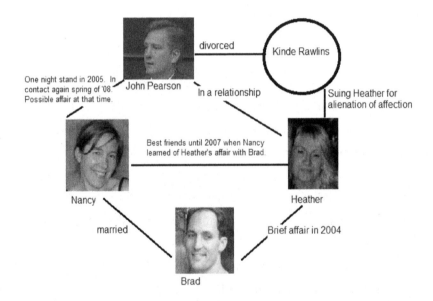

When police asked Pearson about the nature of his relationship with Nancy, he told them they were "friends" and that aside from running into her at a grocery store in June; he hadn't seen her in a year and a half. Later, police received a statement from a witness indicating Pearson had propositioned Nancy.

> "John Pearson allegedly propositioned Nancy after she decided to leave Brad. John told Nancy that he always had a 'thing for Nancy' so why not let us. Kate said this was a verbal incident not a physical altercation." (Detective Dismukes interview with Kate Dunn 9/9/08) [83]

This prompted police to interview Pearson again, approximately six weeks later. This time he admitted that he and Nancy had possibly slept together in 2005. He told them that they never discussed it again and that it only happened one time. He also admitted to police that he'd had recent phone contact with Nancy and that the two met at a coffee shop weeks before Nancy's death. None of this was shared with them during the first interview, yet they didn't ever investigate him as a suspect and there's more.

Detective Dismukes Interview with John Pearson

"I began by asking John if he had developed a 'crush' on Nancy. John told me he and Nancy had a 'fling' at a Halloween party at the Hiller's residence. He stated both he and Nancy were very drunk and Nancy invited him back over to her residence. John said he and Nancy were both naked and they began 'making out.' I asked John if he and Nancy had intercourse. John said he may have, but it was difficult to remember because they were both very drunk. I asked John if he and Nancy had oral sex. He said they may have." (Detective Dismukes hand notes 9/21/08)[84]

Although Pearson said they "may have" had sex, Cary Police actually worded it as confirmatory in a PowerPoint presentation they'd prepared. That indicates that there were likely additional interviews with Pearson but no police notes or recordings to document them.

> "In October 2005, following a Halloween party held at the home of Mike and Laura Hiller, Nancy had intercourse with John Pearson. This incident took place at the home of Brad and Nancy Cooper." (Cary Police PowerPoint 3/10/12) [85]

There was another conflicting statement about the morning Nancy disappeared. During the first interview Pearson said he picked up the kids from Kinde's home but in the second interview he told police that Kinde dropped the children off at his home. When police initially interviewed Kinde, they did not ask her anything about her or John's whereabouts on July 12. She was interviewed again weeks later, at which time police had already received John's alibi information and knew that Kinde was a part of it, yet they never attempted to verify the alibi. They made no attempt to verify his story even though it was inconsistent from one interview to the next.

Kinde was suing Heather Metour for breaking up her marriage with John Pearson. Kinde had been in contact with Nancy about the suit in the spring of 2008. John was married to Kinde Rawlins at the time that Heather and John began the affair. Alienation of Affection suits are permissible in North Carolina.

144

At common law, alienation of affections is a common law tort, abolished in many jurisdictions. Where it still exists, an action is brought by a deserted spouse against a third party alleged to be responsible for the failure of the marriage. The defendant in an alienation of affections suit is typically an adulterous spouse's lover, although family members, counselors and therapists or clergy members who have advised a spouse to seek divorce have also been sued for alienation of affections.[86]

Kinde told police that Nancy seemed very interested in the details of the lawsuit. Was she considering pursuing a suit against Heather as well, or was she possibly worried about being named in the suit herself? There were a lot of discussions going on about the lawsuit.

July 28, 2008 interview with Detective Dismukes (audio transcript):

A. And Nancy said to me, "Are you going to sue Heather?" and she goes, "Are you really going to follow through with that lawsuit?" I said, "Yeah." She goes, "Well, do you mind me asking what you think you're gonna get?" and I said, "I do mind your asking, and I'll let you know when it's over."

Q. So she knew that . . . well . . .

A. She knew I was gonna . . . she knew I was suing her.

Q. But did Heather know or did Nancy have intentions of suing Heather?

A. Well she said to me, "Are you gonna follow through with your lawsuit?" and I said, "I am," and she said, "Well how much do you think you're gonna get?" and she said, "Do you

145

mind me asking that?" and I said, "Yeah, I do mind you ask-ing." I didn't want to tell her that.

There were a series of phone calls between Nancy and John in the spring of 2007 and again in the spring of 2008, just weeks before Nancy's death. Police still didn't consider Pearson a suspect.

Phone calls between Nancy and John Pearson in 2007-08
Nancy to John Pearson
5/1/07 5:41 p.m. (7 minutes)
5/2/07 10:44 p.m. (1 minute)
5/7/08 11:12 p.m. (1 minute)
5/7/08 1:23 p.m. (10 minutes)
5/8/08 9:23 (8 minutes)
5/12/08 9:32 a.m. (1 minute)
6/1/08 5:32 p.m. (8 minutes)
6/12/08 11:52 a.m. (2 minutes)

John Pearson to Nancy
5/2/07 10:44 p.m. (30 minutes)
5/3/07 4:41 p.m. (9 seconds)
5/8/08 12:44 p.m. (5 minutes)
5/16/08 2:50 p.m. (1 minute)
5/16/08 3:20 p.m. (3 minutes)
6/2/08 8:32 a.m. (2 minutes)
6/2/08 9:42 a.m. (1 minute)
6/2/08 9:44 a.m. (5 minutes)

Pearson told police during the second interview that he and Nancy were in contact in May and June because Nancy wanted to discuss the Alienation of Affection suit. He said she didn't want to discuss it by phone, so they arranged to meet at a coffee shop at the edge of town. It is unclear why Nancy would be interested in discussing it with John. It shouldn't have been any of her business unless she was possibly worried about being named in the suit as well. John said they discussed the suit and both were relieved that they weren't involved in it.

Nancy took Katie with her to the coffee shop. This could be important because Katie was born 9 months after the October "fling" between John and Nancy. Was it possible Nancy was confronting him about child support now that she was planning to divorce Brad?

John told police that Nancy invited him to go running that day and they also had a discussion about information that angered him. He further stated to police that Nancy was gossiping about him and that it was a "bullshit lie," but that he couldn't remember what the lie was. There were oddly no red flags to police.

Around this same timeframe, Nancy seemed to be probing Heather for information about the status of her relationship with John Pearson. That could indicate that Nancy was interested and/or involved with him. It is a shame that police didn't investigate that possibility.

Heather Metour interview with Detective Dismukes July 29, 2008

Q. Now, prior to that, when was the last time you had contact with Nancy before?

A. Before the text message?

Q. Um hmm.

A. Um, I was traveling . . . somewhere and she had called me and said, you know, "I haven't heard from you in a while. How are you?"

Q. Um hmm.

A. Um, "Do you know that Kinde got married?", and I thought it was a strange call because I had told her previously that Kinde was getting married.

Q. Um hmm.

A. And um, it . . . *it was almost as if she was fishing for information.*

Q. Um hmm.

A. That would be the best way . . . that's why it felt strange.

Q. What do you think she was fishing for?

A. I don't know. She . . . I have no idea. Uh, to see the status of where I'm at . . . It put me enough on defensive to say, you know, the same as it always is. Some days it's good, some days it's not, sometimes we're on, sometimes we're off.

Heather indicated that she was unaware that John and Nancy were in contact with each other in that May-June timeframe. This indicates that John was hiding his recent contact with Nancy.

"The last time John talked with Nancy was about 1 ½ years ago. This was about the affair." (Detective Dismukes – interview with Heather Metour 7/16/08)

It was an established fact that Nancy and Brad hadn't been intimate since the fall of 2005 while trying to conceive a baby. Police were aware of this information, so when a lab receipt showed that Nancy

148

visited her OB/GYN in April 2008 to request an STD test, they should have been motivated to determine who she had possibly been sleeping with, whether John Pearson or someone else, but they never looked into it. As mentioned, the Coopers' younger daughter was born nine months after John and Nancy slept together, raising the question of paternity. Police should have been interested in verifying paternity as part of the investigation. Brad's attorneys tried to obtain paternity information when they learned that DNA from the children had been requested, but they were unsuccessful. The paternity remains unknown to this day.

During the second interview Pearson told police a very specific running route Nancy would normally take.

> "John said on Sunday (July 13) morning he woke up around 6:00 a.m. and began to walk trails where he knew Nancy had been running before. John told me he knew Nancy ran down Lochmere Drive to Kildaire Farm Road. He stated Nancy would then run to Ritter Park and take back trails over to Regency Park. This is the route John walked on Sunday morning in his attempt to find Nancy. John felt Nancy may have become sick while she was running and possibly passed out in some bushes." (Detective Dismukes narrative #138 8/1/08)[87]

At trial Pearson testified that he did *not* know her running route.

> Q. Do you remember Detective Dismukes asked you if she was taking a trail behind Ritter Park and your response was, "Yes, exactly"?
> A. I misspoke. That's not what I meant.

Q. Can you point out on a map exactly what it was you were describing to Detective Dismukes

A. Yes.

Q. – as being the path she took?

A. No, no. Not that she took.

He testified that the route he described to police is simply a route *he would take* if running from the Cooper's house. He refused to admit that he knew her route, even though he was very specific when he described it to the detective.

Police visited Pearson one more time, not long before trial, and it was only to give him a heads up that the defense considered him an alternate suspect. Police never verified Pearson's alibi, but he took it upon himself to try to establish an alibi "just in case." He asked his ex-wife, Kinde to get a copy of her time card on the date Nancy disappeared. Little did he know, there was no need to worry because police weren't interested in verifying his whereabouts.

Remember that John told police that he was upset with Nancy because she was spreading a "bullshit lie" about him. No red flags were raised here either. This man was admittedly upset with the victim, but police were not the least bit concerned. They maintained their belief that they had the right suspect.

Defense questioning Pearson at trial:

Q. Mr. Pearson, what was it that Nancy said that made you angry?

A. I don't remember the exact words. The gist of it was that I had some feelings for her.

Q. Why didn't you recall that when you were being interviewed by Detective Dismukes?

A. I don't remember. I'm just telling you that's what I remember. The general statement was around that. I – I don't remember exactly what the – you were talking about four people removed, you know, starting with Nancy and I just said "Did you say some negative things?" and asked her about that at the coffee shop and she confirmed, and said she was just upset.

Another oddity about Pearson's second police interview was that he brought up a person named "Michael" from the gym. He suggested that he was strange, that he may have been interested in Nancy, and that police may want to talk to him. It sounded like he was trying really hard to deflect attention away from himself.

John Pearson withheld information from police in an initial interview about a past sexual relationship with the victim; he was potentially the father of one of her children; he knew her running route; he was angry with her about a "bullshit lie," and he tried to direct attention toward "Michael," yet again, no red flags were raised in the shoddy investigation and police would never investigate him as a suspect.

Heather

There are reports that Nancy was openly hostile toward Heather after learning about her indiscretion with Brad in the spring of 2007. Of course, it is difficult to know whether it is true or if it was Nancy telling stories for attention. It was likely the latter, but even the fact that she would tell people things like this indicates that there was a lot of remaining anger over the affair.

> "Nancy was aggressive toward Heather after the affair. Incident at gym where Heather walks into exercise class and Nan announced, the bitch is here." (Dismukes interview with Kinde 7/28/08)[88]

> "When Nancy found out about the affair with Heather, she slapped Heather and told Bella, look at what Ms. Heather did, she is as good as f'ing dead." Dismukes interview with Kinde 7/28/08

Nancy told her daughter's preschool teacher about the affair and also that Heather was not to speak to her children. Heather's son was in the same class.

> "Nancy would tell all the preschool teachers about Brad and Heather's affair." (Detective Dismukes interview with Heather Metour 7/29/08)[89]

> "Nancy told Kathryn that she did not want Heather near her kids. Kathryn said she also kept Heather's little boy at the same time with Nancy's children." (Detective Dismukes interview with Kathy Dorr 8/22/08)

Nancy told several of her friends about instances of Heather stalking her and that she was considering obtaining a restraining order.

152

Jessica Adam's deposition 10/06/08

Q. And do you know why Heather Metour was saying something about a restraining order in the last paragraph?

A. No, I do not.

Q. Did Nancy ever talk to you about she believed Heather Metour was stalking her?

A. Yes.

Q. When did she tell you that?

A. I don't know exactly when. Over the course of a year.

Q. When did she tell you that?

A. Different times things were mentioned.

Q. How many conversations did you have with Nancy about that?

A. About the stalking, specifically?

Q. Yes.

A. Probably a handful.

Q. Based on your conversations with Nancy, what did you believe to be the behavior that she considered stalking?

A. Calling her frequently, and I think there were a couple of times that she showed up at a place that Nancy was at, trying to talk to her. But beyond that I don't know any more.

There was also an email that Nancy sent to Heather in December, 2007, that references the restraining order, so there was clearly a lot of tension between them. There was never any verification of Heather's whereabouts the morning Nancy disappeared. No reviewing phone records, GPS or anything.

"If you feel that I am stalking you, and you feel you need a restraining order, do what you need to do. But you may want to
think of the financial implications of engaging an attorney to
prove that I have in any way physically threatened you or anyone in your family. And may I also remind you, the best case
scenario you will get is a 100 foot bubble, and Lochmere or
what you have lovingly referred to as 'your neighborhood' is a
bit larger than that." (email Heather sent to Nancy 12/12/07)

Nancy's and Heather's relationship seemed to improve slightly in
the spring of 2008, and they began communicating again. Nancy contacted Heather and asked if she would talk to her divorce attorney
about the affair she'd had with Brad; Heather agreed. However, in
light of the love triangle that existed combined with the huge falling
out that occurred between Heather and Nancy, Heather should have
been investigated as a possible suspect.

Nancy's Other Affairs/Romantic Interests
After the Coopers moved to North Carolina in 2001, Nancy became
involved with a man she'd met on vacation in Florida. It was serious
enough that he accompanied Nancy to her twin sister's wedding in
August of that year. Her family wasn't happy about it. She was con-
templating leaving Brad but decided to go home and make things
work. Nancy's friend, Christy Wells told police that their friendship
ended because Christy was tired of being used by Nancy so that she
could talk to the guy in Florida without Brad's knowledge.

"Christy advised that the friendship between Nancy and Christy
ended approximately four to five months after the vacation in Sun-

set Beach, NC, due to Nancy 'using her (Christy)' to talk with the guy in Florida. Christy stated that Nancy would go to lunch with Christy in order to talk to the guy in Florida without the knowledge of Brad Cooper. Christy did not agree with these actions of Nancy and began to ignore Nancy. Christy advised that Nancy was getting advice from friends and the guy in Florida about how Nancy could acquire her citizenship within the United States without the knowledge of Brad. Nancy desired to move to Florida according to Christy." (Detective Young's supplemental report 7/22/08) [90]

It's interesting that Nancy was sneaking around and using her friend to cover for her. Is it possible that the same scenario was going on at the time of her disappearance? Maybe Jessica and Hannah knew more than they admitted, and Nancy was involved with someone. It is also worth noting that Nancy's affair was considerably more serious than Brad's brief affair with Heather, yet the prosecution never referenced it but spent countless days covering Brad's brief fling with Heather. Aside from the known affairs, Nancy had recently been propositioned by some of the men in the neighborhood. One man made inappropriate sexual comments, another expressed his love for Nancy. She was also in recent contact with her former boyfriend, Brett Wilson who she was dating when she met Brad. Certainly police should have considered them potential suspects. Romantic entanglements are normally explored in homicide investigations, but not in this one.

Summaries of Other Possible Romantic Interests[91]
Michael Morwick – Nancy and Mike had recently gone to the beach together, just them and their children. Spouses were not present. A

week before Nancy's death, he expressed to Nancy that he wanted to "fuck Nancy's brains out." Nancy told all of her friends that she was mortified.

Craig Duncan – The Duncans lived across the street from the Coopers. Craig expressed sexual interest in Nancy approximately one month before Nancy went missing. He attempted to hug Nancy and told her that he loved her and that he knew she felt the same. Nancy told her friends the incident disgusted her.

Scott Heider – Cary Police questioned several witnesses about whether Scott and Nancy had a sexual relationship. It is unknown why they considered this a possibility aside from the fact that he and Nancy had run together in the past.

Brett Wilson – Nancy's former boyfriend – she was in contact with him shortly before her death. In an attempt to hide her relationship with him, she deleted emails she'd received. She also texted with him, but the messages were never recovered because Cary Police wiped all of the data from Nancy's phone.

Brett and Jessica Adam

The Adams certainly should have been investigated as suspects considering their actions, lies, false information and inconsistent statements. First let's examine the telephone timeline.

- 9:20 a.m. – Brett Adam phones Jessica's cell phone.
- 9:21 a.m. – Jessica Adam retrieves a voice message.

- 9:36 a.m. – Jessica calls the Cooper's home phone and speaks to Brad, asks for Nancy but never mentions she was due at her house to paint.
- 1:27 p.m. – Brad phones Jessica and asks if she has Carey's number as Nancy hadn't returned and he was getting worried.
- 1:30 p.m. – Jessica calls Hannah and minutes later would state to the police that both of them believed Brad had done something.
- 1:50 a.m. – While Brad was driving around looking for Nancy Jessica made a 911 call to report Nancy missing and stated throughout the call that Brad may have harmed Nancy.

Brett called Jessica's cell phone at 9:20 a.m. then a minute later, Jessica called her cell voicemail for one minute. After that there was no other cell phone activity until 2:14 p.m.[92] Brett Adam didn't have any additional cell phone activity until 2:03 p.m.[93] Jessica didn't attempt to reach Nancy by cell phone while allegedly at the gym or on her way to or from the gym. She testified at her deposition that her cell phone battery had died. If that's true, why didn't she notice during the 9:21 call to voicemail that the battery was low and charge it at that time? She never called Nancy's cell phone at all that morning, though she stated in her affidavit that she had. She was worried enough to call the hospital and then police, but did not call Nancy's cell phone?

Her 9:36 a.m. call to Brad occurred just after she retrieved that voice message from Brett. What if she had just received word that the job was done and she called the Cooper home to see if Brad was home or to see what he would say or if he seemed worried? Jessica told police that she went to the gym with Mary Anderson at 10:00 a.m. She testified that after she arrived home she was unable to eat lunch because she was sick with worry for Nancy. She further explained that she got excited when her phone rang at 1:36 p.m. because she saw it was from the Coopers' *home* phone. Why include that fact? Would she have not been equally excited if it was Nancy's cell phone? Was she really feeling ill because she was waiting for word that Nancy was missing and the call from the Coopers' home phone meant it was time for her to swing into action – time to place the 911 call pointing the finger at Brad? She was breathless the whole way through the call, yet parts of it seemed rehearsed as though she was reading from bullet points.

There were also several red flags associated with the 911 call. Tracy Harpster, an expert in the field of 911 call analysis wrote an interesting article titled *911 Calls and Statement Analysis – Is the caller the killer?*[94] It examines the probability of the caller's guilt based on the characteristics of the call. For example, offering extraneous information, not requesting assistance for the victim, acceptance of the victim's death, self interruptions and being polite and patient are all considered red flags with a strong likelihood that the caller is the killer. Of course a thorough analysis is important, but certainly the 911 caller should always be looked at.

The 911 call was lengthy because of all the extraneous information she provided. If she wanted immediate assistance she would not have needed to accuse Brad of anything or describe the fact that Nancy was pretty. She would not have had to tell police that her friend also suspected Brad. This was all extra information that wasn't going to help police find her friend. She didn't beg for them to help find Nancy. She was concerned with what police could do for *her*. If she was genuinely worried, shouldn't she have gone searching for her instead of creating a huge hysterical scene at the Coopers'? She also seemed to be accepting of Nancy's death. She yelled, "I know he did it!" in front of all the friends and neighbors that afternoon.

Jessica began steering the investigation immediately, even telling people not to talk to police. She remained in close contact with police throughout the investigation and supplied false information. She pressured everyone to write negative affidavits against Brad, she told police Brad knew how to automate a call. Why was she so intent on forcing a case against Brad instead of letting the investigation progress on its own? Many times people do this to deflect attention away from them.

Jessica's relationship with Nancy was intense and could also be described as unstable. She was *desperate* to be Nancy's friend when they first met, she literally cried at the possibility that her husband may have sent Nancy a text message and she wanted Nancy's dress after her death.

Then consider Brett Adam. Did he place the 9:50 p.m. call to Nancy? If it was Brett, it is significant because that was the last call Nancy received the night before she was murdered. As mentioned previously, Jessica told police that *she* placed the call, but there were inconsistencies from one interview to the next regarding the context of the phone call.

First interview:

"Jessica told me she spoke with Nancy again via telephone around 10:30 p.m. (Friday) to see if Nancy wanted to come over to her house. Nancy told Jessica that she had had too much to drink at the party and she did not think it would be a good idea for her to go to Jessica's house right now. During this second conversation <u>Nancy again told Jessica that she would see Jessica sometime around 8:00 a.m. on Saturday.</u> (Detective Dismukes 7/12/08)[95]

On July 22, the purpose of the call changed, and there was no longer any confirmation of plans for the following morning.

"Jessica told me the main reason she called Nancy at 10:30 on Friday evening was to check on her at the neighborhood cookout. She stated the neighborhood is extremely dysfunctional and Nancy recently had an unpleasant experience with one of the neighbors. (Detective Dismukes 7/22/08)[96]

It changed again during her deposition in October 2008.

Q. What did you talk with her about?
A. How the bathing suit that she and I had bought wasn't working out.
Q. Anything else?
A. No. We laughed and I asked her how she was doing. She sounded well, and I had invited her to come over to my house if she wanted to, if she felt like she wanted to leave the neighborhood and she said she wasn't, that she was OK.

So she told three different versions of the 9:50 phone conversation with Nancy. This should have been a red flag. At trial she testified that they did not confirm any painting plans for the next morning. The circumstances of how the call was placed also varied. This was Jessica's description of the call.

> "I called Nancy because my friend Mary Anderson had decided to come back to my house from our pool and have a glass of wine with me. And I – Mary and I thought, "Well, _we'll_ call Nancy." And I called her to invite her to see if she was interested in joining us." (Jessica Adam, Brad Cooper trial)

During Jessica's deposition in October, 2008 she described how she came to use Brett's cell phone to place the call. Note that Cary Police supplied Jessica with all her phone records to review in anticipation of her deposition, so she had an opportunity to see that 9:50 call from Brett's phone so she would be able to explain the call.

> Q. And why did you use your husband's cell phone?
> A. I think because I just didn't feel like getting up to get the phone and he was sitting across the room from me and he always wears his cell phone.

Mary Anderson told police a completely different story than Jessica about the 9:50 call.

> "I had just pulled into Jessica's driveway and she was standing on her front porch because she didn't want me to ring the doorbell and wake up the kids. She was on her cell phone or on her regular phone. I would say it was a regular phone, um, saying . . . and she said she was talking to Nancy who was at Diana's party or gathering, whatever it was. Um, yes. So yeah.

161

When I walked in, she was on the phone with her and that's
when . . . at that point I knew – you know, she had said that
Nancy was gonna come over in the morning and paint because
she . . . we were talking about moving some furniture out of the
dining room." (Mary Anderson Cary police interview 8/22/08)
97

Mary first stated that she overheard the conversation outside, then
moments later it changed to "when I walked in." Jessica said they
were together when she phoned Nancy; Mary said Jessica was already
speaking to Nancy when she arrived. Jessica said she borrowed Brett's
phone because he was sitting across from her. Mary said it was a
regular phone and that she wasn't even there when the call was
placed. Also, Mary makes no mention about Nancy being invited to
join the two of them for a glass of wine as Jessica described at trial. If
Jessica placed the 9:50 call, why so many inconsistencies? Why are
her and Mary's versions so different? Why wasn't this a red flag to
police? The question remains – Did Brett Adam actually call Nancy?

Brett Adam also made those strange blog posts referring to a
Google map to aid in the search for Nancy and then later the reference
to searching gullies when they were searching for a live person. He
also pressured Craig Duncan not to write an affidavit in support of
Brad. His testimony about the morning of July 12 was inconsistent
with Jessica's. He said that Jessica woke him at 7 a.m. to move furniture because Nancy was due to arrive to paint, but Jessica told police
they didn't even wake up until 8 a.m. There were so many different
time frames when it came to the alleged painting plans. Jessica lied to
police, had inconsistent stories and somehow seemed to know Nancy

was dead when she called them, but she became their star witness instead of a suspect.

The possibility of a random perpetrator was also ignored as they failed to investigate reports of a strange van in the neighborhood and reports from two separate witnesses about seeing two Hispanic men in the van. It's clear there were many possible suspects but no one but Brad was ever considered. Many potential leads were completely ignored. The decision to ignore the possibility of alternate suspects highlights the extent of the tunnel vision that influenced every aspect of the investigation. Detective Dismukes testified that Brad was the only suspect in the investigation. Detective Young testified that it was not important in this case to determine whether or not Nancy had any affairs, past or current, yet the Cary Police Department dedicated extensive resources and time to attempt to discover any improprieties of Brad, even asking Interpol for assistance.

{ 15 }

Fabricated Evidence

Now it's time to scrutinize the "evidence" that was presented in this case. In each instance, prosecutors, whose salaries are paid with our tax dollars, intentionally misled the jury by misstating facts. Police conducted a dishonest investigation, but prosecutors are supposed to be the gate keepers. They decide which cases to try based on *sufficient* evidence, not fake evidence.

> A prosecutor has the responsibility of a minister of justice and not simply that of an advocate; the prosecutor's duty is to seek justice, not merely to convict. This responsibility carries with it specific obligations to see that the defendant is accorded procedural justice and that guilt is decided upon the basis of sufficient evidence. ~ Rules of Professional Conduct [98]

Unethical prosecutors try to classify fabricated evidence and unfounded speculations as **circumstantial evidence** and the jurors often fall for it, but they are being fooled. Circumstantial evidence must be fact based. It is a string of <u>facts</u> that when added together can over-whelmingly suggest that a person is guilty of a crime. Fabricated evidence does not count. Another author wrote a book about this case and stated there was a "mountain of evidence." The mountain was comprised of fake evidence.

A quick example of legitimate circumstantial evidence would be a credit card receipt that places a person near the scene of the crime. It is a tangible piece of evidence that doesn't *prove* the accused commit-ted the crime, but it could be classified as *fact*-based circumstantial evidence. Then, if there are several more suspicious facts, they could be combined to make a compelling case of guilt. It is distinguishable from *fabricated evidence*, which is not fact based, but built upon mis-statements and speculations, as you will soon see.

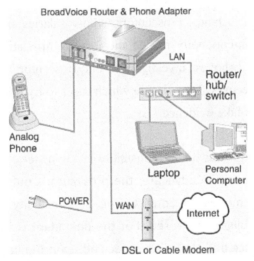

The 6:40 a.m. Phone Call

Police had a theory that Brad murdered Nancy just after midnight when she returned home from the Duncans' party. They had a big problem though. According to Brad, and verified phone records, Nancy called Brad on his cell phone while he was en route to the grocery store and asked him to pick up Naked Green Juice for their daughter, Bella. The 6:40 a.m. call lasted thirty-two seconds and was *verified* both through the land line record and Brad's cell phone record. There was a lot at stake as the police chief had already declared this an isolated incident. They didn't want to admit they were wrong for suspecting Brad, but proof that Nancy called Brad at 6:40 a.m. crushed their theory. They were left scrambling to try to refute this persuasive evidence of Brad's innocence, and they formulated a theory that Brad somehow automated the phone call.

Brad was a VoIP (Voice over Internet Protocol) engineer with Cisco. Police believed that his background would allow him to somehow *make it appear* that a call was placed from his home land line phone to his cell phone without leaving any trace. Think about that for a minute. They were using his area of expertise against him by making a bold assumption that simply having expertise in a field implies that he *likely* used that knowledge in a nefarious manner to commit a crime.

Police received a lot of "helpful" information from Nancy's friends. Jessica and Hannah told police that Brad had replaced their home system with a Cisco phone and that Nancy complained about it because of clicking sounds. Jessica speculated that he did this so he could listen in on Nancy's calls from work and could also remotely disconnect her phone calls. There is no evidence that anything like that ever occurred, but the trial testimony included *speculation* about it. Brett Adam referenced the belief that Brad was using his expertise to monitor phone calls and included his ability to remotely initiate calls.

"Jessica had experienced multiple telephone calls with Nancy that were inexplicably disconnected. She asked me whether Brad could be responsible for this and whether he could be listening in to their conversations. I believe that Brad installed a VoIP phone system in his home such as the Cisco system which allowed him to remotely initiate calls, terminate calls, and monitor call activity." (Brett Adam's affidavit)

However, at the time of Nancy's death, the Coopers had a standard V-Tech cordless phone for their land line. Nancy had told Brad several months prior to her death that she didn't like the Cisco phone, so Brad replaced it. That detail didn't stop police from pursuing the idea that Brad must have automated the call . . . somehow. Police received a tip about Brad's ability to "spoof" a call from *NC Wanted*. Cisco engineer Anthony Laaper posted the tip, and Detective Dismukes met with him in October 2008.

"Brad knows what he is doing with phones. He is *that* good. Anthony told me about writing scripts and that Brad has the capability on his computer to write a script and make a phone call from his computer to a cell phone." (Detective Dismukes interview with Anthony Laaper 10/14/08)[99]

So the idea was established, and Cary Police ran with it, convinced that Brad must have automated the phone call with his computer. They presented the claim that he "could" accomplish this in a Cary Police PowerPoint document, presumably presented to the DA office, and possibly later to the Grand Jury.

"He stated that Nancy called him at 0640 hrs on the morning of the 12th of July, but information was learned from his job and later his own statement that he could make a call remotely as if the call came from his residence." (Detective Daniels, Cary Police Power-Point 10/25/08)[100]

Could They Prove It?

Police sought an expert in the field of VoIP – Cisco VoIP Engineer, Paul Giralt. Detective Young first asked Giralt about the capabilities of the Coopers' land line phone.

> Detective Young: "Is there any method for completing the call from the residence to the cell phone using a V-tech 6.0 cordless telephone system with answering machine? Note: I've attached a copy of the owner's manual to this email."

> Paul Giralt: "After reading the attached copy of the owner's manual, assuming the phone does not have any other 'hidden' capabilities that are not documented in the instruction manual, there does not appear to be any way to use the V-tech phone to call a cell phone other than manually dialing the number from one of the V-tech handsets and being in physical proximity to the V-tech base station." (Cary police email regarding spoofing call with home phone 8/23/08)[101]

That turned up empty, so next they explored the possibility that Brad's Cisco phone in his home office could have automated a call. Paul Giralt informed Detective Young that the Cisco phone was unable to automate a call because it would need to communicate with the servers at Cisco to function. However, he suggested that a server could be set up in the home if a specific type of router was in place – one with an FXO (foreign exchange office) port to communicate with the land-line phone, but there wasn't one in the house.[102] Nonetheless, police decided to run with the idea.

Giralt described how this special type of router could be connected to the home phone line in place of the standard phone and using a command known as "csim," the router could *appear* to pick up the phone, wait twenty-three seconds and then hang up. However, there was a huge problem with this theory. The 6:40 a.m. call lasted thirty-two seconds, and the maximum time the "csim" command will last is twenty-three seconds.[103] Again, it didn't seem to matter to police and prosecutors that the timing eliminated this as a possible method to "spoof" the phone call. They continued the speculation game. Cary Police prepared a PowerPoint presentation (likely for the prosecutors), outlining how the router could be used to spoof a call.

Cary Police PowerPoint 8/6/08
Method #1 CSim with Router Hyper Terminal

- A Cisco engineer, who has extensive knowledge of Cisco programs, computers and cell phones, advised there is a "hidden" diagnostic command (CSIM start) within Cisco software which allows a router to place a telephone call.
- This telephone call is made from the router via a telephone line of an individual's choice by making a connection to the router.
- The most basic way is to access an application known as HyperTerminal via a laptop connected directly to a physical cable.

- Using the basic method, a delay between 1 second to 136 years could be used to instruct the router to delay the telephone call being made.
- This method would result in a telephone call being made from a residence to a cell phone according to telephone records.

Method #2 CSim with router Telenet

- The Cisco engineer advised that the telephone call could be made via access to router using applications containing "telenet" or "secure shell" instead of by use of direct access to the application (HyperTerminal).
- Access to the application of telenet or secure shell would not leave a record within a computer or wireless device which could be used for this method.
- The method discussed above does not require a drop down box, such as is commonly used to access a website such as "www.tarheelblue.com."

Cary Police presented this theory to the prosecution, knowing that Brad didn't have the necessary equipment to accomplish this, and that even if he did, the 6:40 a.m. call lasted too long, making the supposition impossible. That should have been the end of this, but it didn't stop police. Their entire case was predicated on the belief that Nancy was already dead when the 6:40 call was placed. They were desperate to find proof that Brad automated the call. Next, Detective Young asked Giralt about the possibility that Brad may have spoofed a call through the Cisco Call System. Nope.

"There were no calls between the RTP VTG or Galway, Ireland Communications Managers and any Cisco IT production Communication Manager cluster, from 6 a.m. through 7 a.m. ET. This confirms that none of the Cisco IT managed Meeting Place servers placed a call through the RTP VTG Alpha or Galway Communications Manager clusters from 6 a.m. through 7 a.m. EST." (Paul Giralt 8/23/08) [104]

In September 2010 with the trial approaching, Detective Young began searching for a VoIP expert who was not a Cisco employee. He was still hoping to find a sound method for spoofing the call, but he never did. Police never did find the proof they needed, but that didn't stop them from pursuing Brad as the only suspect. The prosecution would just have to use a lot of smoke and mirrors at trial to convince the jury that Brad "could have" and therefore "must have" spoofed the call.

Routers
Detective Young checked the routers out of evidence on 9/24/10 for one month. If Brad's computer was used to generate a call, the router logs would have provided proof. No mention was ever made of any analysis or results in any of the discovery. When asked about the routers at trial, Detective Daniels testified that he was unaware of the reason the routers were signed out because Detective Young was tasked with that responsibility. Detective Young testified that he signed them out for Agent Johnson of the FBI, and had no knowledge of what was done with them. FBI Special Agent Johnson and Officer Chappell both testified that they never requested the routers for testing and that they never looked at them as part of the investigation.

The defense made several requests for the router logs, but never received anything. The routers were very important for two reasons. First, to prove that Brad didn't "spoof" a phone call with his computer, as alleged, and second, to analyze computer activity around the time that the computer was vulnerable to tampering. Did they find exculpatory evidence that proved that Brad did not use his computer to automate a phone? Did they hide something favorable to Brad? Someone lied about the routers. They were checked out for a solid month for some reason.

Trial

Even though no proof of a spoofed call was found, the prosecution forged ahead with their speculation game at trial. They called Paul Giralt to testify generically about all the ways one *could* automate a phone call. The testimony was very detailed, very boring, and it lasted several days. The defense cross-examined the witness, and it was quickly determined that a) there was no equipment in the home capable of generating an automated call by computer, and b) there was no call on the Cisco managed call system between 6 – 7 a.m.

The prosecution clung to the "csim-start command theory" and tried to sell it to the jury during closing arguments, but it just wasn't plausible because of the twenty-three second time-out. I guess they believed that throwing out a bunch of technical methods would somehow convince the jury that the prosecution actually had something. They had nothing, but the jury apparently bought the notion that Brad's mere expertise in the field was circumstantial evidence that he spoofed the call. They were wrong to not force the State to provide proof of their claim.

Detective Daniels' Testimony

Q. Everything you're saying about the 6:40 a.m. phone call being set up, or however you want to characterize it, is pure speculation?

A. I don't believe its speculation. I believe that I was shown several ways it could have been done, and that's what I was basing it on.

Q. You don't have a single log entry from any router saying that that's what happened, do you?

A. No, I don't, no.

Q. You don't have any kind of phone records that indicate that's what happened, do you?

A. No.

Q. You don't have any expert that can come in here and say that is what happened, do you?

A. No, I don't.

Rebuttal Testimony

State witness Greg Miglucci testified that Brad acquired a 3825 router in the winter of 2008 and that it was "missing" from his inventory records. A 3825 is capable of automating a phone call; however, they failed to prove that any such router was hooked up at the time of the 6:40 a.m. call. They also tried to suggest through this witness that the 3825 router was now missing from Cisco's inventory, implying that Brad never returned it and that he must have used it to automate the 6:40 phone call and then disposed of it. First, everyone who works at Cisco knows that they keep poor inventory records and that equipment comes and goes from the site all the time. Keep in mind that the trial occurred three years after the murder. We can't expect Brad to be accountable for a piece of equipment from three years earlier. Aside from that, the defense discovered that the "missing" 3825 router referenced by Miglucci actually had a manufacture date of September 2008 (well after the July 12 alleged spoofed call). The "missing" router was a red herring, and Miglucci's testimony was meaningless. Even if there was proof of a missing router, the length of the call remains an issue that can't be explained away because the 6:40 a.m. call lasted thirty-two seconds. Further, even if the 6:40 call *had* been within the 23 second limit, there should have been evidence of the call on the server, Cisco logs or Brad's computer, but despite three years of searching, nothing was found.

Note: This was <u>not</u> circumstantial evidence. If they had proof that Brad automated a phone call, then it would be circumstantial evidence. Speculation does not count.

When police couldn't find any evidence that Brad spoofed the call, they should have re-evaluated their theory and actually began investigating the murder. They never proved that Brad spoofed the call, so they were obligated to give him the benefit of doubt but they refused to admit they were wrong. The 6:40 a.m. call from Nancy is one of the strongest indicators of Brad Cooper's innocence.

The Dress Deception

The dress Nancy wore to the party was important because according to the detectives' theory, Nancy was killed soon after she arrived home that night. Would investigators find evidence that she'd been killed in that dress? Would there be signs that a struggle occurred? On the evening of July 12, a canine search was organized, and police needed an article of clothing that Nancy had recently worn. Brad told Detective Young that he believed Nancy had worn a **blue** summer dress to the party. After Detective Young's search came up empty, he asked Brad if he was sure about the clothing. Brad confirmed that he was fairly certain but decided to go across the street to get Craig and Diana Duncan to help. They had hosted the party, so he was hoping they would remember what Nancy had been wearing. Brad brought them back to the house and, in Detective Young's presence, asked Diana if she remembered what Nancy had worn to the party. Diana responded "a **black** dress." Detective Young quoted her statement in his hand notes. That search also came up empty, so they used one of Nancy's shoes for the canine search.

The next morning, when Detectives Daniels and Young went back to the Coopers' home to ask Brad more questions, he informed them that he'd found the dress. He went upstairs to grab the blue-green Ella Moss dress so he could show it to the detectives. Note that photos taken by police on July 12 show that the dress was actually lying in a laundry basket all along, but Detective Young somehow managed to overlook it.

The detective's inability to find the dress would be twisted and used to make Brad appear guilty. Young claimed that Brad "threw him off" by describing the dress as *blue* when it was, in his opinion, green. The color of the dress was described by witnesses in many different ways—blue, green, blue-green and teal, so it was ridiculous that police and then the prosecution used Brad's description to portray him as a liar, but they did.

Nancy Cooper's Green Dress in Laundry Basket

Diana Duncan cast suspicion on Brad by telling police that he intentionally erased her memory about what Nancy had worn to the party by deceiving her about the color.

Diana's trial testimony:

A. I think my ability to remember what she was wearing that night had been compromised.

Q: How so?

A: It just – it's like the memory had been replaced.

Q: And was there a reason you felt that way?

A: I felt that Brad did it on purpose.

Q: Okay. How so?

A: By coming over and saying let me – "Help me find the black dress she was wearing . . . and going through and looking at a ton of black things."

Of course she was lying, because Brad never said the dress was black. *She* did. Diana didn't inform police about Brad's attempt to "replace her memory" about the color until July 21, despite having interviewed with them about this very subject a week earlier.

Diana's many descriptions to police:

❖ 7/12/08 at 8:13 p.m. – "green with black print" (Detective Dismukes typed the narrative on 7/21/08)

❖ 7/12/08 at 9:00 p.m. – "black" (Detective Young's hand written notes)

❖ 7/13/08 – Interview with Detective Young – described the dress in great detail but *could not recall the color.*

❖ 7/21/08 – Interview with Detective Dismukes – Told him *Brad tried to confuse her with the black dress talk.*

It was utterly ridiculous to suggest that Brad was intentionally deceiving anyone about the color of the dress or trying to erase Diana's memory, but that was the type of thing prosecutors presented. Honestly, why would Brad have even informed police that he'd found the dress the next morning if he was trying to hide it? Wouldn't it have been smarter to just avoid bringing it up at all?

Was the dress washed?

Although Detective Daniels' *initial* police notes contained no record that the dress had been washed, both Detectives Young and Daniels testified that when Brad gave them the dress, it smelled "fresh" like Downy and that Brad told them he had washed the dress. Further, they testified that Brad also mentioned that there was a stain on the dress, because he remembered Nancy being concerned that it was noticeable at the party.

Note: <u>Brad did tell them about the stain but never told them he'd washed the dress.</u>

Detective Daniels recorded a simple statement about the green dress in his hand notes during the July 13, 2008 interview.

> "Green Dress, what she was wearing in hamper in her room."[105]

. . . 6 months later Detective Daniels *changed* his report for that date.

> "He ran upstairs and retrieved the dress. It <u>smelled with a strong scent of Downy.</u> When asked about this he stated that he had washed her dress (which according to all parties was very unusual to do. Brad was not known to wash clothes at all). It was noted that the dress was in the hamper in her bedroom. (Detective Daniels' narrative #9 12/3/08)[106]

The detective "updated" his report to bolster the case against Brad. It made Brad seem guilty to have washed the dress, right? He altered his report and then testified about the "dress washing, Downy scent." In all, Detective Daniels posted thirteen additional details to his July

13 report as late as six months later. This was fraud. Had the interview been recorded, police wouldn't have been able to get away with this. This is why one should never talk to police without an attorney present.

Since Brad mentioned a stain on the dress, police decided to question some of the party guests again to verify his statement. According to police, none of the guests knew anything about Nancy spilling anything on her dress; therefore from the detective's perspective, Brad must have lied about the stain and used it as an excuse to wash the dress (even though he didn't wash the dress!). At trial several witnesses testified that they were unaware of Nancy spilling anything on her dress. Just because Nancy didn't inform guests, did not mean she didn't spill something, but they were trying to show that Brad was lying about the stain.

CCBI collected the dress into evidence July 16. They met with Cary Police on July 20, and again on August 1. Police requested no testing on the dress. Finally on August 7, Detective Young was told by his superiors to have the dress tested. Why wouldn't he have submitted it for testing immediately? It should have been a huge priority to determine if there was evidence that she had been murdered in that dress or evidence that the dress had been washed to hide a crime. Were police worried it would not contain incriminating evidence?

Detective Young was told to submit the victim's dress for analysis by his superiors. Since we discussed not submitting the dress when he and I met on Friday 8/1/08 at Cary PD, he was calling to inquire what section needed the dress for analysis. (SBI Agent Amanda Thompson's report 9/9/08)[107]

An SBI worksheet dated September 5 <u>notes a grease stain on the dress that is not included in the final report</u>. There is no mention of the stain in any of the discovery.

"<u>One small grease-like stain</u> was observed on the front of the dress which seeped through to the inside of the dress. The stain tested negative for blood and did not appear to be consistent with a bodily fluid when viewed with the ALS." (SBI Agent McMillan's report 9/5/08) [108]

SBI Agent Ivy McMillan testified that there were deodorant streaks in the underarm area of the dress and also described the stain she had discovered during her examination of the item. This was proof that police lied about Brad's statement that he had washed the dress. The detectives pretended the SBI results didn't exist. They made not a single reference to the stain in any of their reports, and then at trial they refused to acknowledge the factual evidence.

<u>Detective Daniels' Testimony</u>:
Q. You note that, with respect to the green dress, the July 13th interview with Brad, that Brad noted Nancy had spilled something on the dress, but no one at the party recalled a stain on the dress?
A. That's correct.
Q. But you recognize that the SBI identified a stain on the dress?
A. <u>I wouldn't classify it as identifying a stain</u>. They identified something small. I didn't see what he was saying as the stain being something small that . . . even at one point, it couldn't be

found. So I would stick by that statement that he was the only one who recognized the stain.

Detective Young denied even knowing the results of the SBI testing because it didn't support the fabricated story.

<u>Detective Young's trial testimony</u>:
Q. You are aware at this point that the dress has what appear to be deodorant stains under the arm?
A. No sir.
Q. You were not present for the SBI Agent McMillan's testimony?
A. No, sir.
Q. Do you recall having a conversation with Agent McMillan of the SBI about the stain that she found on the dress?
A. No, sir.

The detectives were deceitful, Brad was not. They spent an enormous amount of time concocting an elaborate story to suggest that Brad hid, washed and lied about the dress, but none of it was true. It was the prosecution's responsibility to acknowledge the facts, but they did not. They picked up the ball and ran with it. They were aware that Brad didn't hide the dress, and they were aware of the SBI testing that proved the dress hadn't been washed, but instead of being forthcoming with the truth, they acted unethically by eliciting false testimony to make Brad look suspicious.

Note: This is definitely not circumstantial evidence because none of their claims about the dress were factual.

Brad's "Missing" Shoes

The prosecution presented false evidence again by claiming that the shoes Brad was wearing the morning of July 12 were missing. Police asked Brad about his clothing during an interview on July 14 that occurred just after he had been out searching for Nancy. Brad stood up at that point and said, "Pretty much this, but with a pair of jeans." He was wearing shorts at the time but had on the same black shirt he had worn the morning of July 12. Police never asked him about his shoes or clothing again nor requested them for evidence. When they obtained a search warrant on July 15, Brad's clothing and shoes were not even mentioned. [109]

Three years later at trial, they claimed that the shoes had never been found . . . unbelievable. Assistant District Attorney Boz Zellinger asked Detective Young, "Have you ever been able to find the shoes defendant was wearing the morning his wife disappeared?" Detective Young responded, "No." Brad's attorney cross-examined Detective Young about the shoes.

> Q. Did you ever ask Brad for the shoes he was wearing that morning?
> A. No.
> Q. Is it referenced anywhere in your notes that you searched for the shoes or were unable to find the shoes?
> A. No.

Despite the detective's confirmation that he had never searched for the shoes, the prosecutor continued to question the detective on re-cross. "Did you ever find the shoes Brad was wearing that morning?"

Detective Young again responded, "No." There was no clarification that he never *searched* for them and that he had the opportunity to request them from Brad but neglected to do so. It was improper for the prosecutor to mislead the jury this way.

Soil samples from Fielding Drive were compared against soil from a pair of Brad's Nike shoes found at the house, and there was no match, so they decided to claim that Brad disposed of the shoes he'd worn that morning. The morning of July 12, Brad made two trips to Harris Teeter. Surveillance video shows that on the first trip, he wore a pair of athletic shoes, and the second trip, he wore some type of sandal. Since he wore different shoes on the second trip to the store, it was easy for the State to make the claim that he disposed of the athletic shoes. However, there is absolutely no evidence to support the claim.

Soil testing wasn't done until two years after Nancy's death. ADA Boz Zellinger requested for Detective Young to arrange the testing with the North Carolina Program for Forensic Sciences. Young and Zellinger met with Heather Hanna on June 25, 2010. They requested a comparison of soil samples obtained from the location of the body, the Coopers' home, Lake Johnson and Lake Lochmere. Detective Young delivered several items to Hanna for testing – Nancy's flip-flops, Brad's boots, Brad's Saucony athletic shoes, Brad's sandals, Brad's slippers, an oval rug and Brad's Nike athletic shoes. She ended up testing only one item—Brad's Nike shoes. She did not test any of Nancy's shoes to see if she ever ran in the Fielding Drive area. It's likely that the shoes they sent for soil testing were in fact the shoes Brad was seen wearing in the store surveillance video. Had they found a soil match, they would have offered it as proof that he was at Fielding Drive that morning.

Hanna testified that she identified what "appeared" to be white mica clusters on both Brad's shoes and Fielding Drive soil samples. On the surface, it sounds incriminating; however, it yielded no meaning-ful information because Hanna was unable to chemically analyze the particles due to their inherent structure. This meant that they may not have even been mica at all, and having not analyzed them, it was im-possible to know the precise composition.

Next, the Defense questioned Hanna, and it was revealed that there were other types of mica that she *was* able to chemically analyze—low and high magnesium particles from the soil samples. The high magnesium particles from Brad's shoes were most consistent with particles from Lake Lochmere and *inconsistent* with Fielding Drive. The low magnesium particles from Brad's shoes were also incon-sistent with Fielding Drive. They were not compared with Lake Lochmere, and it was noted that they were possibly from an unknown location. These conclusions were revealed only during cross-examination. The prosecution cherry-picked from the evidence and opted to exclude testimony about the low and high magnesium sam-ples even though the results were much more accurate than the white mica clusters. The cluster samples were nothing more than visual comparisons. It would be like comparing two hair samples visually, soliciting testimony that they looked similar and then leaving out tes-timony that DNA testing excluded the accused.

Since soil from Brad's shoes did not match the Fielding Drive soil, the prosecution made the purposeful decision to present more fabri-cated evidence – the suggestion that Brad disposed of his shoes. ADA Boz Zellinger repeated, "The defendant's shoes are missing!" over and over throughout the trial and into closing arguments, despite the fact that police never searched for or asked for the shoes that Brad was wearing that morning. It is undeniable that both police and prosecutors were unethical and dishonest in their characterization of this evidence.

Note: This was not circumstantial evidence. They fabricated a story about missing shoes.

Nancy's Running Shoes

The prosecution next attempted to show that Nancy couldn't have gone running that morning, because her running shoes were in the home. They did this knowing that a pair of her running shoes was never found. When police were unable to locate the dress Nancy had worn to the party, they decided to use her shoes for the canine scent. There were two pairs of running shoes on the shelf in the laundry room – a newer pair of Saucony's and an older pair of Asics. Brad told Detective Young that there was also a *missing* pair of Saucony's. This statement was verified by the detective at trial during cross-examination.

> Q. Am I correct that it says, "Obtained from laundry room shelf one additional pair of running shoes, female . . . noted no "void" for "third pair" of running shoes wife would have been wearing?"
>
> A. Yes, sir.
>
> Q. Mr. Cooper told you that there was a third pair of running shoes that his wife could have been wearing?
>
> A. I don't recall that statement, but I do have it in quotes.
>
> Q. When you say you do have it in quotes, that to you indicates what, sir?
>
> A. That indicates a statement that I was documenting at the time.

Note: Detective Young believed there should have been an empty spot (void) for the third pair of shoes. He was already suggesting Brad was lying about a third pair of shoes.

ADA Zellinger elicited a false statement from Detective Young –

> ADA Zellinger: Did the defendant ever tell you about a third pair of shoes on July 14th?

> Detective Young: No.

Zellinger then asked "When I say "third pair," did the defendant ever tell you Ms. Cooper went out running in a different pair of shoes than were in that house?" The detective lied when he responded, "No, sir." His hand written notes confirmed that Brad had informed him about the missing pair of shoes. ADA Zellinger was aware of the quote in the detective's notes "no void for third pair of shoes," so he was intentionally misleading the jury. Additional documentation further supported Brad's statement about the missing Saucony shoes.

- ❖ "Brad also told me that Nancy would normally wear Saucony running shoes." (Detective Young narrative #10 7/12/08)
- ❖ "Nancy last seen in light blue running shoes" (Cary Police release 7/12/08 7 p.m.)
- ❖ Additionally, Detective Young referenced the shoes in a search warrant.

187

"On Sunday, July 13, 2008 Brad Cooper advised affiant that a pair of running shoes, which Brad described as dark blue in color 'Saucony' running shoes were missing from a shelf within the laundry room in the residence." (Detective Young's search warrant)

Nancy purchased the missing shoes in September 2006. Jessica Adam provided police with a photo of her and Nancy taken in November 2006 at a Turkey Trot race. Nancy's missing Sauconys were noted in the photo, which obviously proved that she didn't return the shoes. However, after efforts to find the shoes came up empty, Detective Young visited The Athlete's Foot store where she'd purchased the shoes, hoping to find evidence of a return. When that turned up empty, Detective Young submitted multiple court orders for financial records and received hundreds of pages of documents in hopes of finding evidence of the returned shoes, but no evidence of a return was found. The shoes were not returned, and they have never been found.

One may suggest that perhaps Nancy threw away the missing Saucony's. That wasn't typical of Nancy because she still had the Asics she had purchased in 2005. Further, Detective Young's notes indicated that Brad referred to Nancy's size 9 ½ Asics as her "oldest" pair of shoes and her size 10 ½ Saucony's as her "newest" pair. [110]If there were only two pairs of shoes he would have referenced them as the "old pair and new pair."

The prosecution continued their spin at trial. Detective Young was extremely evasive when questioned about his extensive search for Nancy's missing shoes. He tried to deny that the store found no evidence of a return. The defense had to make him read his statement of that fact from his own affidavit. Prosecutors misled the jury by eliciting lies from the detective, and they stated that Nancy's running shoes were in the home even into closing arguments, never acknowledging the missing pair of Saucony's.

Note: This is not circumstantial evidence. If Nancy's only running shoes were in the home, it would be circumstantial evidence consistent with the police theory, but they didn't have that. They resorted to unethical tactics to present the illusion that the missing shoes never existed.

The 32-Digit Pass Code

Throughout the trial, prosecutors asserted that Brad placed a 32-digit pass code on his cell phone to try to keep investigators from accessing his data and further that he (or someone close to him) deleted most of the data from the phone. They did this with *full knowledge* that Brad's employer, Cisco, utilized two forms of software on company-issued cell phones to protect proprietary information. Goodlink Mobile Guardian Shield allowed Cisco to remotely decommission phones when someone's employment was terminated or a phone is lost or stolen. It essentially wiped out all Cisco data linked to the phone.

Credant is encryption software. If an incorrect 4-digit pass code is entered, it will prompt one to enter a 32-digit code to unlock the phone. *The prosecutors knew this*, but it didn't stop them from suggesting that something sinister happened with Brad's phone, and the judge allowed them to do it.

The prosecution elicited testimony from witness David Fetterolf who described seeing Brad's attorney hand the cell phone to Brad's mother at a hearing that occurred before Brad's arrest. The implication was that Brad's attorney played a role in the cell phone data being deleted. The judge allowed the testimony despite a defense objection, even with full knowledge that there was documentation from Cisco

189

describing the process of how the software removes the data when an employee is terminated.

Facts about Brad's phone:

❖ Cary Police confiscated all computers and electronic evidence on July 16, 2008, except for Brad's Blackjack cell phone. It is unclear why they didn't seize it at that time, especially in light of the 6:40 a.m. call from Nancy on Saturday morning.

❖ When police finally took custody of Brad's phone, they made no attempt to review data from the dates surrounding Nancy's disappearance and death. They sent the phone to an FBI forensic expert to be analyzed but never instructed him to look at the contents within that time frame.

❖ Defense attorneys offered to give prosecutors the code to get into the phone, but they declined.

❖ The phone was sent to the FBI to be analyzed a little over a year after Brad's arrest. FBI Agent Charles Wilmore testified that he was unable to get into the phone, and was prompted by Credant software to enter a 32-digit code. He notified the Cary Police Department which then contacted Cisco for the code. Cisco supplied the code 10 weeks later.

❖ After Agent Wilmore entered the code, he was able to gain access to the contents. While there was some data on the phone, most had been wiped out by the Goodlink software shortly after Brad's arrest. There were still some voice and text messages on the phone.

❖ If investigators were so concerned with the data on the phone, why didn't they seize it early in the investigation, and why didn't they request information specific to those dates when they finally had it analyzed? It was another sign of a shoddy investigation.

❖ State witness Chris Fry from Cisco testified that the 32-digit pass code was a normal function of the Credant software.

❖ Detective Jim Young testified that although he received the email from Cisco about the 32-digit code and how the software worked, he didn't know if that information was "accurate." He apparently felt he couldn't trust it, even though he relied on Cisco for evidence of the alleged spoofed call.

❖ Prosecutors also alleged that the lifetime usage of the phone appeared to be just **31 minutes** – suggesting that someone (Brad) reset the phone since phone records indicate there was much more usage on the phone. In reality, the phone had **31 *hours*** of lifetime usage. This was more misleading and false information put in front of the jury.

Misleading testimony (ADA Zellinger questioning Detective Young):

> Q. And speaking of Mr. Cooper's cell phone, I believe you testified on direct it had a 32-digit code to unlock it; is that accurate?
> A. Yes, sir.

Technically Detective Young wasn't lying because there *was* a 32 digit code on the phone, but it was completely misleading because *Brad didn't place the code on the phone*. The detective and prosecutor were fully aware that Brad did not place the code on the phone, but they wanted to present the illusion that he had. It was extremely unethical and dishonest. ADA Zellinger elicited additional false testimony from Detective Young about the lifetime data usage found on the phone.

191

Detective Young: When we looked at the phone within the past few weeks, I noticed that there's a screen that stated something about a reset, but it dealt with the life – the life total calls or the life of the phone. And it had what appeared to be a 31 minute life – overall life for the phone, pertaining to the call history.

ADA Zellinger: You've seen the defendant's call phone records. Is that consistent with what you know of the Defendant's calling on that phone?

Detective Young: No, sir . . . not based on the cell phone records. Thirty one minutes would not be consistent.

Note: This is not circumstantial evidence. It is fraudulent evidence. Brad didn't put a 32 digit code on his cell phone and the phone contained 31 hours of usage; not 31 minutes.

Brad's Route to Harris Teeter

On the morning of July 12, Brad made two trips to the Harris Teeter store. Brad was questioned about the *route* that he took to the store on each trip during his custody deposition in October 2008. Brad said he believed he took the <u>southern route</u> on trip one and the <u>northern route</u> on trip two. He said he recalled being at the traffic light when he received the call from Nancy. That would have been the northern route.

After reviewing the store's surveillance videos, Detective Young *incorrectly concluded* that Brad had taken the southern route both times. Police used the information to discredit Brad's claim that he received the call from Nancy at the traffic light; therefore he must have lied about the phone call. It was revealed during cross-examination that the detective was *wrong*. Brad *did* take the southern route on trip one and the northern route on trip two. Young brushed it off as a mistake in the way he viewed the camera angles.

Prosecutors probably didn't realize until mid-trial that Detective Young was incorrect about the location of the car as it entered the parking lot, yet nothing was done to correct this. They never stated that it was all a mistake and that the cameras actually confirmed Brad's described routes. It had to be cleared up during defense questioning. The prosecution spent *hours* questioning Young about the store cameras and his observations about Brad's car in the videos and ultimately, it added nothing except to prove that once again Cary Police were wrong. Prosecutors were wrong.

Note: This is not circumstantial evidence. It did nothing but waste the court's time.

The Bed Did Not Look Slept In

The evening of July 12, Brad gave detectives permission to take photographs of the house. Detective Daniels later recorded in his notes that Nancy's bed didn't appear to have been slept in. The bed was quite wrinkled, and the blankets were messy and rolled down, so why would he record that observation? Was he using more false information to build a case against Brad? Is it possible that he didn't realize someone was going to take a photograph of the bed? Detective Daniels testified that he sat on the bed to demonstrate to Detective Dismukes what a slept-in bed *should* look like. No one documented how the bed appeared *before* the "demonstration." The jury was simply to accept that the bed looked undisturbed when he initially saw it!

The incompetence was magnified because the bedding was collected and sent to the SBI to be examined for bodily fluids and a possible fiber analysis. Detective Daniels didn't alert anyone at the SBI that he had contaminated the evidence. Did he really sit on the bed, or did he get caught lying about the actual state of the bed?

There were no negative consequences for contaminating potential evidence in a homicide investigation or for failing to document before-and-after photos of the bed. In all likelihood the detective never sat on the bed, but was forced to come up with a story to explain the fact that the photo was inconsistent with his notes. Additionally, Detective Dismukes' notes indicate that Brad was with the detectives when the photos were taken because he was showing them around the house. They wouldn't have been able to do the "demonstration" in his presence.

Note: This is certainly not circumstantial evidence. No explanation is necessary.

Green Juice

The question of whether or not Bella drank green juice was important to police because they viewed it as part of Brad's alibi, and they wanted to find inconsistencies with his story. Remember that Brad told

them that Nancy asked him to pick up
Naked Green Juice for Bella during the
6:40 a.m. call. Since police theorized
that Nancy never "actually" called Brad
that morning, they questioned every aspect of the call, to include the context of
the conversation.

Police believed it was unusual that
Nancy would request green juice for a four-year-old child, and since
police understood that Brad often drank the juice himself, they asked
all of Nancy's friends and family if they ever saw Bella drink it. It
would support their theory if they could show that Bella didn't drink
green juice. At trial, all of the State's witnesses responded similarly –
that Bella would drink the juice if it was served to her but that they
had never heard her ask for it. That is a little ridiculous – the suggestion that she liked it but would never request it.

Prosecutors presented a bunch of store receipts showing that Brad
purchased green juice when Nancy and the girls were out of town to
support the theory that the juice purchased on the morning of July 12
was for him, not Bella. However, Nancy did in fact purchase green
juice for Bella on July 2 while they were on vacation. Her sister, Krista testified that Bella spotted the juice in the grocery store and
requested it but that she would only ask for it if she saw it in the grocery store. Right . . . she would only ask for it *if it was in the store*, not
if it was in the refrigerator at home! Again, it was ridiculous testimony.

When Detective Daniels was questioned by the defense about the
green juice investigation, he stated that it was of no significance to the
case. He refused to admit that they were looking at it to discredit the

6:40 phone call. The fact is the juice was found in the Coopers' refrigerator when police searched the house, so clearly the juice wasn't for Brad. Prosecutors stated in closing arguments that Brad probably bought the juice because he was thirsty from all of the murder clean-up. It was improper for prosecutors to elicit testimony from multiple witnesses to try to suggest that Bella "wouldn't ask for it" when they knew that she did request it and she did drink it.

Note: This was not circumstantial evidence. Bella drank green juice.

Hay

Officer Hazelzet testified that he observed a piece of hay on a rug in the entranceway of the Coopers' home on July 15. The significance is that hay was present at Fielding Drive, so it could have been transferred to the home by Brad the morning of July 12.

On July 15, 2008, at approximately 3:40 p.m., Detective Daniels told Officer Hazelzet to request Brad's permission to enter the home and remain until the search warrant was ready. Brad granted him permission to enter and then went upstairs to take a shower. While Brad was upstairs, Hazelzet *allegedly* spotted a piece of hay on a rug in the entranceway. He did not photograph the hay; he didn't collect it for evidence; he didn't collect the rug, and he didn't inform a single person that he had seen it. He spoke to Detective Daniels at 5:00 p.m., so he had ample opportunity to inform him about the hay, but he did not. Police continued to enter and exit throughout the day. Hazelzet never mentioned it at that point either.

CCBI was at the house that same day and specifically told to look for hay. They reported that none was found. Hazelzet testified about his alleged observation even though there was absolutely nothing to document it. Photos from July 12 show no presence of the hay he would have observed. In Hazelzet's initial report on his activities on July 15 he never mentioned observing any hay in the home. He amended his typed report twenty months later to include observing hay in the home. Amazing to recollect a detail like that two years later and take the time to add it to one's notes.

Note: This is not circumstantial evidence. If they had photos or some type of proof beyond the officer's word, then it could be classified as circumstantial evidence. The testimony contributed nothing.

Scratch Marks

Detectives Daniels and Dismukes testified that they observed scratch marks or rub marks on the back of Brad's neck the afternoon of July 12, but no one else saw them and they neglected to document them with photos. Brad was wearing a short sleeve shirt on the afternoon of July 12, and there is a photo of him sitting outside—no visible scratches. Brad attended a press conference on July 14—no visible scratches. There are surveillance videos of Brad at the Harris Teeter store the morning of July 12, again—no visible scratches. CCBI was told to swab for DNA and photograph any injuries on Brad July 15. No scratches were observed on his neck. Brad noticed that police mentioned the scratch marks in a July 16 search warrant, so he arranged for someone to photograph the back of his neck. No visible marks were seen.

The following are Detective Daniels' many descriptions of the scratches. Note that they are all attributable to his observations on July 12.

- "Scratch on back of neck" (7/12/08, hand written notes)

- "red marks on Brad's neck, left side – five fingers" (8/6/08)

- "Several red marks/scratches on the rear of his neck, looked to be like a person's fingers sliding across the rear of his neck." (Cary Police PowerPoint)

- "rub marks" (trial testimony)

It's likely the description evolved to "rub marks" at trial when all the imagery was pointed out to the detective and not one photo or video revealed any scratches or marks on Brad's neck. The only person who corroborated Daniels' claim was Detective Dismukes, yet his initial narrative from July 12 makes no mention of scratch marks.

"As I sat down to talk with Brad I noticed he had a band aid around the tip of his middle finger on his left hand. I also noticed Brad was wearing a baseball hat, shorts and a t-shirt. Brad sat across from Officer Hayes as we began to talk. At 1605 hours, my interview with Brad I noticed Brad was wearing a wedding band. (Detective Dismukes **narrative #10** 7/12/08)[111] **Note:** No mention of scratch marks.

"At 6:35 p.m. Detective G. Daniels requested that I introduce him to Brad Cooper since I had already spoken with him earlier. I complied with Detective Daniels' request and walked him over to where Brad was sitting on the front steps with a neighbor. I introduced Daniels to Brad Cooper. Daniels asked Cooper if we could go inside and talk. Brad seemed a little annoyed that

Daniels wanted to speak with him but he walked inside anyway. Brad walked in front of us through the front door when Daniels stopped me and pointed out that Brad had some <u>red markings on the back of his neck.</u>" (Detective Dismukes narrative #89 7/12/08)[112]

Note: He referenced marks when he typed up his second narrative.

Police photographed every room of the house on July 12 and never bothered to take a photo of the alleged scratches on Brad's neck to document their observation. They took a photo of Nancy's bed but not Brad's neck? Neglecting to document something with a photo makes it easy for police to make up information about things they allegedly observed.

Ducks

Police showed Hannah and Jessica photos taken of the Coopers' home on July 12 to see if they could identify anything out of order. Jessica told police that when she was at the Cooper home on Friday, July 11 (was she  even there?) she noticed that a set of three decorative ducks was missing from a foyer table and bamboo shoots were missing from a vase in the foyer. This was very important to the State's case because it supported their theory, that Nancy was killed just after returning home from the party. The missing decor was *evidence of a struggle* that they desperately needed to prove their theory. The struggle would have occurred in the foyer, and ducks may have been broken!

But again, Jessica was wrong and made police and prosecutors look incompetent. The ducks were actually packed away in a box all along because Nancy had packed up a lot of items in anticipation of her move. There were boxes all over the house, but police never looked for the ducks; instead they ran with this as *"evidence of a struggle,"* and so did the prosecutors until the defense presented the ducks at trial. Brad's mother had seen the ducks while helping Brad pack up the house, and luckily they were still around. ADA Howard Cummings yelled at Carol Cooper, "You realize you just made our witnesses look like a bunch of liars?!"

Detergent

The type of detergent the Coopers used was important to police because Brad purchased Tide brand detergent the morning of Nancy's disappearance. Like the green juice, this was part of the alibi police wanted to break down. The implication was that if Nancy was already dead when Brad made the trip to the store, he wouldn't have known what type of detergent to buy. If he bought the wrong type of detergent, this would support their theory.

Based on police records, it appears that they only asked Jessica Adam what type of detergent the Coopers used. She told them that she believed they used the brand, All Detergent. She was wrong. Store records verified that the Coopers had thirty purchases of Tide, dating back years. This became one of the "inconsistencies" noted by Detective Daniels while viewing Brad's deposition. He made a notation, "Tide, not All," because he believed Jessica Adam instead of Brad. His suspicion was wrong.

Trunk

Detective Daniels testified that Brad's car trunk was "showroom" clean, implying that Brad had the body in the trunk, removed it and then vacuumed it to remove all evidence. There was a shop vacuum sitting in the Coopers' garage. Police never collected it to analyze the contents, showing their lack of planning and incompetence.

Detective Young testified that he never had any opportunity to look inside the trunk on July 12 when in fact Brad had given police free rein of the house. SBI Agent Macy testified that there was dirt and debris in the trunk. When asked about Agent Macy's observation, Detective Daniels made the ridiculous assertion that the dirt and debris must have gotten there *after* he viewed the trunk. Additionally, the first responders wrapped Nancy's body in a sheet before transporting it to the medical examiner. The sheet was examined and fibers were found, but none of them matched the fibers from Brad's trunk.

The Garage

Prosecutors questioned countless witnesses about the condition of the Coopers' garage. It was well known that both Brad and Nancy parked their cars in the driveway because the garage was filled with lots of toys and various other junk. The State asserted that the garage was straightened up enough so that Brad could fit his car inside to place the body in the trunk. Based on the evidence photos, there was still no room for a car in the garage. There was a large Barbie Jeep in the garage and a ladder and other objects taking up space.

Jessica Adam testified that when Brad picked the girls up on Tuesday (that same week), Nancy and Jessica were discussing Jessica's offer to help organize the Coopers' house, including the garage. Brad said that he had already organized the garage, and Nancy said that she still could not fit her car in the garage. Gary Beard, the Coopers' exterminator, testified that the garage was very cluttered when he treated the home that same week. Detective Dismukes testified that he believed a car could fit in the garage at an angle. None of this matters because there is no proof that a car was in the garage anytime on July 12, the day that Nancy disappeared.

None of the "evidence" described pointed toward Brad's guilt, yet it was misstated as such by the prosecution over a span of six long weeks. They wasted time, they wasted money and they attempted to trick the jury into believing there was something incriminating there. The State presented a lot of non-evidence to prove the point that Cary conducted a thorough investigation but it was not thorough, it was micro-focused on Brad.

{ 16 }

Destroyed Evidence

Digital evidence can provide investigators with crucial information – voice messages, text messages, emails, address books, photos, social media and even GPS. During the course of the Cooper homicide investigation digital evidence was permanently destroyed by Detective Young when he wiped all data from Nancy's Blackberry cell phone. There's no question that the data was wiped, the question is—was the evidence *intentionally* destroyed or was it accidental? Let's review the facts.

Brad gave the cell phone to police the day Nancy disappeared. As stated previously, Detective Dismukes placed it in his desk until it was entered into evidence July 25 so there was no chain of custody up to that point. Police also neglected to access it to try to find Nancy while it was still a missing person's case. Brad's attorneys, Howard Kurtz and Seth Blum sent Cary Police a letter of preservation to ensure that all digital evidence in the case would be carefully handled.

This is a notice and demand that critical evidence in this matter exists in the form of electronic data contained in your computer systems, cellular phone and/or Palm, Treo, Blackberry or other PDA devise(s) used by Nancy Cooper and/or Bradley Cooper, including but not limited to any CPU, laptop, flash memory device, floppy disc, hard drive, digital voice disc, Subscriber Identity Module (SIM) cards or other electronic media be immediately preserved in its present state and that there be no spoliation or alteration of data. This evidence must be immediately preserved and retained until further written notice of the undersigned. This request is essential, as a paper printout of text contained in computer files or SIM cards does not completely reflect all information contained within the electronic files. Additionally, the continued operation of the computer systems identified herein could likely result in the destruction of relevant evidence due to the fact that electronic evidence can be easily deleted, altered or otherwise modified. The failure to preserve and retain the electronic data outlined herein in this notice constitutes spoliation of evidence. (July 30, 2008)

Three days after receiving the letter, on the Saturday afternoon of August 9, 2008, Detective Young erased *all* data from Nancy's cell phone. Detective Daniels had tasked Detective Young with performing a "forensic preview" on the Blackberry phone. Detective Young had never had training in digital forensics. Cary Police has officers knowledgeable in that field, but he didn't seek their assistance. It is mind boggling that the lead detective would make a request for an inexperienced officer to preview an electronic device when they had just received a letter reminding them to take special precautions to properly preserve the evidence. Young claimed that in an attempt to do the preview, he contacted an AT&T representative with the subpoena compliance department and he then submitted a court order to receive a Pin Unlock Code, known as a PUK code. Note that a court order is not necessary since the code can be found on the AT&T website. He said he was given instructions on how to use the PUK code by the customer service representative. He did not ask to speak to a technician or write down the instructions. He didn't even ask for the representative's name for his record.

Ten days after allegedly (there is no record) receiving the instructions, the phone was wiped of all data. From memory he did what the representative told him to do. He actually claimed he was instructed to enter an incorrect code ten times. If one does an internet search for "How to erase a Blackberry," the instructions are consistent with what Detective Young described. Warnings are also clearly referenced on the AT&T website.

Note: If you enter the wrong PUK code 10 times in a row, your SIM card will be invalidated, and you will need to purchase a new SIM Card.

As a precaution, the user is also prompted to enter the word "blackberry" and he still proceeded until he finally got to the final warning screen that states that data will be erased and he clicked "OK". Young followed the exact instructions for "how to wipe a blackberry" and then simply said, "The AT&T representative told me to do that.", but that's not all. He also destroyed the SIM card! Erasing the contents of the cell phone and invalidating the SIM card requires two *separate* processes.

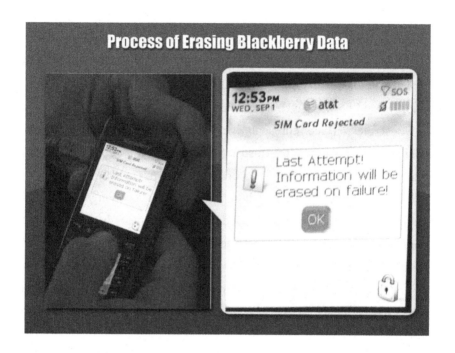

Process of Erasing Blackberry Data

Each process requires the password to be incorrectly entered 10 times with warnings along the way. Approximately six weeks after wiping the phone, he requested a search warrant for the (already destroyed) phone. He gave the phone to Detective Thomas who confirmed that there was no remaining data. After that he waited *eleven* months to notify Brad's attorneys about what happened to the phone. At that point the privacy policy had expired, making it impossible to ever receive the detailed phone records which would have included text messages, social media information, address books and more. Had he informed them even two months earlier, they could have requested the information from the provider.

This letter is to provide a brief synopsis of the examination performed relating to a black 'Blackberry Pearl' cellular telephone. During the course of the investigation regarding the homicide of Nancy Lynn Cooper, I attempted to access the cellular telephone by obtaining a 'puck code' from AT&T to complete a 'forensic preview'. In an attempt to execute the 'puck code', which was obtained via a court order from AT&T, I completed steps to 'unlock' the cellular telephone, which were provided to me via telephone by an AT&T representative. These steps failed to successfully 'unlock' the cellular telephone and in fact 'wiped out' any and all information contained on the cellular telephone.

Detective Young's explanation isn't even logical because although a PUK code will unlock a phone, without a password it would still be impossible to do a forensic preview. The only way Detective Young would have been able to view the contents would have been through the use of a Cellebrite or other similar forensic tool.

After receiving notification that the phone had been erased, the defense arranged for Ben Levitan, an expert in digital evidence, to examine the letter, the explanation of what happened and the phone itself. Mr. Levitan was surprised to find that not only had the phone been wiped, but the SIM card had also been destroyed. According to him, September 29 was the date when the SIM card had to have been destroyed since it was no longer updating the time and date. That would have been after the search warrant was issued. He testified at trial that he had *never* seen evidence destroyed in this manner during an investigation.

Mr. Levitan's summary[113]:

IV. SUMMARY AND CONCLUSION

Given all of the forgoing, it is my expert opinion that:

1. Detective Young erased Nancy Cooper's BlackBerry intentionally;

2. Detective Young erased Nancy Cooper's BlackBerry's SIM card intentionally;

3. The erasure of Nancy Cooper's BlackBerry's SIM card occurred in September, 2008, not August, 2008, as he claims;

There was no justification for Detective Young to have touched the phone, and this really highlights how corrupt the investigation was. It is very possible that Cary Police destroyed evidence favorable to Brad, or maybe they were attempting to preserve Nancy's reputation. Perhaps they did it out of spite after receiving the warning letter from the defense. "Don't touch the electronic evidence? We'll show them what happens when they tell us what to do!"

Prosecutors claimed that the destruction of this evidence was *insignificant* since they already had the phone records. As mentioned, a privacy policy had expired, making it impossible to ever retrieve detailed records that included the content of text messages and more.

Nancy's V551 Cell Phone

There is evidence that police also wiped Nancy's older cell phone. Detective Young obtained a search warrant for the phone on April 16, 2009, and then signed the phone out of evidence on April 30. On June 11, he noted that there were 250 contacts present on the card on the phone. He gave the phone to Detective Thomas to perform a forensic examination and oddly *no* contacts were found. What happened to the

250 contacts? The phone was placed back into evidence on June 15 and there were no further attempts to retrieve the data from the phone.

Detective Thomas's trial testimony

Q. Turning your attention to State's exhibit 316, which is Ms. Cooper's old V551 phone, is that correct?

A. Yes, sir.

Q. You have some training in working with cellular phones?

A. No.

Q. Okay. No expert training in working with cellular phones?

A. No.

Q. Okay. No expert training at all in how to do forensic exams on phones?

A. No.

Q. Do you have computer forensics training?

A. Yes.

Q. And at that time you used what was called a Data Pilot?

A. Yes, sir.

Q. And the information that you received from the Data Pilot stated initially 250 contacts?

A. I don't recall on the Data Pilot. It reported different than the Cellebrite.

Q. Did you take notes about your examination?

A. I just noted no data was found.

Q. And you're unaware as to whether or not it stated anything about contacts being on the phone?

A. That's correct.

Q. Did you test the V551 with the Cellebrite?

A. Yes.

Q. When was that?

A. I don't recall the date I did that.

Q. Do you have your notes with you?

A. I do. I don't have any notes on that, best I recall.

Q. Detective, you did a forensic examination of the phone and you did not take any notes?

A. That's correct. I took notes on the initial exam.

Q. Are you aware of Cary Police having protocols requiring documentation of testing?

A. Specific protocols, no.

Q. Do you believe that that is an appropriate forensic technique to employ without documenting your actions?

A. It depends on the situation.

Q. Did something come up? Did an emergency come up that prevented you from being able to document what it is you had done in your examination?

A. Not that I'm aware of.

Q. Did you take photographs of the device as you were documenting the examination?

A. Not that I recall.

Q. Did you have witnesses with you when you were documenting the examination?

A. No, sir. Not that I recall.

Q. Did you simply turn the phone on and flip through it?

A. Not that I recall, no.

Q. But you said the phone was on when you actually used the Data Pilot with it, correct?

A. You have to turn it on.

Q. And once you've got a telephone that's running, you can navigate through menus, can't you?

A. Yes.

Q. Did you check how many contacts were on the phone just by looking on the phone?

A. No, sir.

Q. Did you look to see if there were any photographs on the phone?

A. No, sir.

Q. Did you look to see if there were any voice messages on the phone?

A. No, sir.

Q. Text messages?

A. No, sir.

Q. Emails?

A. No, sir.

Q. Is there a reason why you didn't?

A. Yes. If I can't retrieve data with my tools, it's up to the investigating officer to look through the phone.

Q. But you did a second exam on the phone at some time later?

A. With new equipment.

Q. With new equipment, and you still were unable to find information on the phone?

A. Exactly.

Q. And to the best of your knowledge, it violates no protocol for you to navigate the phone, does it?

A. As far as I'm aware, no.

Q. And you simply didn't.

A. I had no reason to.

The apathy exhibited by this police officer was shocking. Nobody seemed to care that the contacts were gone. No effort to retrieve the contents was taken and no one seemed to care that evidence was destroyed during the course of a homicide investigation. Chief Bazemore referred to the destruction of Nancy's Blackberry phone as a "mistake." She never ordered an investigation into the destroyed evidence to determine how it happened and what measures could be implemented to prevent a reoccurrence. There were no negative consequences to Detective Young for this action. Chief Bazemore, the mayor and the town manager congratulated the detectives for a job well done at the end of the trial. The mayor was reelected later that year. Detective Daniels even received an award for his contribution to the Cooper investigation in 2008.

Excerpt:

The nomination also highlighted his informal leadership, mentoring and community service. In 2008, Detective Daniels served as lead detective on three homicide investigations. These homicides occurred over an eight month period and required numerous man hours and investigative work. Although many detectives and officers worked on these cases, two detectives (Jim Young and Adam Dismukes) worked with Detective Daniels extensively. According to Sergeant Byrd, "Detective Daniels not only provided tremendous leadership and direction with these cases, but served these detectives as a mentor and an informal leader. Both of these detectives have grown professionally because of working with Detective Daniels. [114]

Retired Detective George Almond and 2008 Winner
George Daniels

Daniels received an award after conducting a dishonest investigation. Under his supervision evidence was destroyed, witness statements were manipulated, reports were altered, alternate suspects were ignored, chain of custody was ignored and who knows what still remains unknown about the botched investigation.

{ 17 }

Brad's Affair and Others Alleged

Brad had a very brief affair with Heather Metour approximately four years prior to Nancy's death, but the prosecution made it a focal point of the case. Heather and Nancy were best friends from shortly after the Coopers moved into the Lochmere neighborhood. They were together constantly. They ran together, had meals together and drank wine in the evenings. Heather was married to Scott Heider at the time, and the couples would often get together for dinners. Brad also worked with Scott at Cisco.

In May, 2007 Pam Letts, a mutual friend of Nancy's and Heather's, confronted Heather with an ultimatum. If she didn't tell Nancy about the affair, Pam would. Heather told Nancy about the affair, it ended their friendship, and Heather was out of the Lochmere social circle. At that point Brad denied the affair and it's difficult to know if Nancy believed him or not but the marriage seemed fine based on some of the things they were doing. For example, the couple was house hunting in the fall of 2007.

Brad denied that he'd slept with Heather because he worried it would destroy their marriage, but he finally decided to tell Nancy the truth in early 2008. He told her that the indiscretion occurred several years prior, that he was sorry that it happened and that he regretted that he'd kept it from her. He didn't want to hurt Nancy. In all, the "affair" had lasted only a few short weeks, and Brad realized it was a mistake. He wanted to remain married and sought a marriage counselor. The couple attended a joint counseling session and then individual sessions a week later, but there were issues with rebuilding trust and Nancy made the decision to separate from Brad.

There was a lot of innuendo at trial that Brad had additional affairs, but the claims had no substance. Nancy suspected that he was having an affair with a woman from his MBA program but there was never anything throughout the investigation to confirm that. Police began speaking with a man from Brad's MBA program shortly after Nancy went missing. According to police records, Joseph D'Antoni initially told them that Brad shared a room with a woman on a trip to France in 2007.

> "Joseph D'Antoni, who was a classmate of Brad's in the NCSU MBA program, advised that Brad met a female, Celine, on a trip to France. Brad and Celine stated in the same hotel room the entire week. (Cary Police PowerPoint 8/5/08)[115]

The truth is that Brad and his classmates stayed in a dormitory that week, not a hotel and further there is no statement from D'Antoni that corroborates the police PowerPoint script. At trial, D'Antoni testified that he never saw Celine in Brad's room or witnessed her entering or leaving the room. It is puzzling that Cary Police documented the statement about Brad sharing a room with Celine when D'Antoni's email to Detective Young as well as his signed affidavit completely contradicted that.

Defense cross-examination:

Q. And, Mr. D'Antoni, I'm showing you what's been marked as Defendant's Exhibit 66. Do you recognize this document?

A. Okay, yeah. This is the affidavit I sent to Detective Young.

Q. And in this document, does Detective Young ask you whether Celine Busson ever spent the night in Brad Cooper's dorm room?

A. Yes.

Q. And what was your answer to that question?

A. "Not that I'm aware of."

Q. Now, I'm showing you what's been marked as Defendant's Exhibit 67. And do you recognize this document?

A. Yeah. It's an email from myself to Detective Young.

Q. And in this email, isn't it an accurate statement that you say, and I quote: "I'm sure she never spent the night."

A. Yes. My statement was "I'm sure she never spent the night, but he may have spent the night at her place." But I don't recall, or I can't testify to that.

So again, this was nothing more than speculation. There is no evidence that anything inappropriate occurred. Brad denied that any affair took place aside from his indiscretions with Heather Metour. Nancy told a lot of her friends that there were "several" affairs but again, there is no proof whatsoever. She told some bizarre stories about a woman approaching her about an affair that she'd had with Brad. There are a few different versions of the story. It seems illogical that anyone would approach a stranger and say "Hey, I had an affair with your husband.", so more than likely these were made-up stories, but of course they were included in the trial.

"Carrie stated she remembered Nancy telling her about a mysterious phone call she received from a female who confessed to having an affair with Brad. Nancy told Carrie the female never identified herself and did not say anything about the affair. Carrie told me this phone call occurred sometime in April 2008. Carrie stated she did not know who the female caller could have been." (Detective Dismukes narrative #145)

"And she said she was someone who was planning to have an affair with Brad, and she said that she would be happy to come forward and provide evidence of that. And Nancy said to her – thanked her very much and she said, 'You know, it really doesn't matter. You can if you want, but it really doesn't matter. I know there are affairs. It really doesn't matter.' And it was left at that, and she told me about it, and I said, 'You know, Nancy, in case this down the road becomes something you're going to need, you should take that information. Why wouldn't you?'" (Donna Rentz deposition)

Garry Rentz's testimony

A. We talked about an incident, and this is I'm going to say mid-early February toward the 10th, Nancy phoned me, and said that she had been approached by a woman in Harris Teeter who recognized Nancy from a photo. In fact, it was the photo that Mr. Kurtz used on the upper left hand of his bulletin board on opening day to show the family. And that photo was taken at NC State. And Donna and I were there when it was taken, and we took pictures too, and so did NC State, but they published it in their news magazine.

Q. Right.

A. And this woman recognized Nancy from that?

Q. Nancy is telling you this?

A. This is Nancy telling me.

Q. Okay.

A. And said that the woman approached her in Harris Teeter and said "I hear you're divorcing Brad. If you're interested in evidence, I'll be glad to provide you with some."

Though the above stories are very far-fetched, the idea that Brad had multiple affairs was thrown around in court quite a bit. It was prejudicial, but the judge allowed all of Nancy's stories to be retold by dozens of witnesses. Nancy's affairs were never mentioned until the defense case.

Affairs are often brought up in spousal murder cases because it points to motive – means, motive and opportunity, right? However, in this case, Brad's indiscretion should not be considered motive since it had been over for quite some time. It wasn't even really an affair since they only slept together one time. He was not looking for a way to be with Heather, therefore there was really no need to discuss this at trial, except to explain how it ultimately led to the decision of the couple to separate. The affair was unjustly used against Brad Cooper. It was character assassination. There is a tendency to suggest that since one is capable of having an affair, they must be capable of murder. The affair was discussed excessively at trial. The prosecutors even questioned the Coopers' exterminator about the affair. Every single friend and family member was questioned about it, so dozens of people repeated the same thing over and over. How was this in any way providing the jury with evidence that Brad was responsible for Nancy's death? It wasn't. If the prosecutors had solid evidence, they wouldn't have had to resort to tactics such as this.

{ 18 }

FBI's Selective Computer Analysis

When the FBI examined Brad's computer, they found evidence that Brad had his website set up so that Nancy's emails would automatically be forwarded to the website. While prosecutors made it sound horribly invasive, the truth is that the email and website both were used for family-related communication such as school, activities, family photos and things like that. Nancy's email account, nanner@nc.rr.com, was also used for paying household bills. The computer Nancy used had no password. It was in the common living area, and Brad and Nancy both routinely used the computer.

Brad set up the website to track his Ironman training and also to post and share family updates and photos of the children. He never used the email that was included with the website, and he was not spying on Nancy. If she had wanted a private email address, she easily could have created a different one, and actually, evidence of a separate email could have been on the cell phone that police destroyed. Since there was no password on the family computer, her email was accessible to both of them at all times, and it was not an issue.

The prosecution made a big deal out of Nancy's having received the separation document and the appearance that Brad had "intercepted" it, but Nancy sent it to his email. There were no privacy violations. Nancy's sister actually had the "nanner" account labeled as Brad and Nancy Cooper because it was a family account.

Nancy's Facebook Account

When Brad and Nancy wanted to share photos with friends and family, they simply emailed the photos. Brad had no idea that Nancy had a secret Facebook account. The defense team had no motivation to request information from Facebook because as to Brad's knowledge neither Nancy nor he had ever used Facebook.

The FBI conducted an analysis of all computers and wrote reports of their findings. Their reports failed to mention that there was a Facebook account in use. The prosecutors withheld from the defense copies of the computer images for almost a year. Once the defense did obtain the images they soon discovered the Facebook account. However, by the time the account was discovered it had already been deleted from the Facebook system. The defense did manage to obtain a fragment of Nancy's Facebook page that was cached on Google. It showed that some of Nancy's friends and neighbors were linked to her account.

It can be assumed that either Nancy's friends or the FBI informed the police of the Facebook account however, nowhere in any hand notes or written report does the word Facebook appear. By withholding the information and computer images the prosecution destroyed any chance of the defense of finding who Nancy was communicating with or more importantly the contents.

It's obvious that even the FBI was involved in an effort to find everything they could to make Brad appear guilty, but intentionally obscured and ignored any action to determine who Nancy had been communicating with to determine possible suspects in the case. The entire effort was 100% focused on Brad from beginning to end.

{ 19 }

Spoliation and Tampering

The **spoliation of evidence** is the intentional, reckless, or negligent withholding, hiding, altering, or destroying of evidence relevant to a legal proceeding. The theory of the spoliation inference is that when a party destroys evidence, it may be reasonable to infer that the party had "consciousness of guilt" or other motivation to avoid the evidence. Therefore, the fact finder may conclude that the evidence would have been unfavorable to the spoliator.[116]

Often in criminal cases, the prosecution and defense experts offer opposing opinions about forensic evidence. Evidence such as blood spatter, time of death, cause of death or even fingerprints can be subjective. In this case, the evidence of tampering is not subjective. It is not open to differing opinions. Computer expert Jay Ward discovered multiple irrefutable signs of tampering on Brad's IBM ThinkPad computer. The defense's second expert, Giovanni Masucci, discovered even more signs. The State experts never searched for tampering, and therefore when asked by the prosecution, "Did you *find* any signs of tampering?" they were able to respond that they hadn't, because in fact they never looked. It was similar to the "missing shoes" testimony.

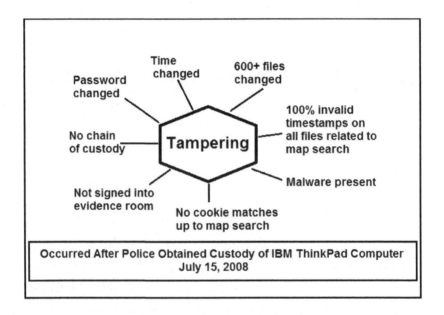

The spoliation took place beginning on July 15. Police arrived at the Cooper home at approximately 3:00 p.m. Brad left home at 5:20 p.m., and at that time the computer was running, connected to the wireless network with no browser open, and Brad was still logged on. Police didn't shut down the computer until 27 hours later.

Signs of Tampering

1) Passwords

Brad's user account "bracoope" was suspiciously absent from the SAM (Security Account Manager) file, which is the database that stores passwords. Instead there is an administrator account and a disabled guest account.

Excerpt from Jay Ward's Report:
Brad was participating in Cisco's Vista beta program, and it was confirmed that the local administrator password for the Vista beta program does not match the password on the machine. The only other password ever used by Cisco was also entered, with every capitalization and number combination available. These tests failed. The Administrator password on the IBM ThinkPad is not the current Cisco administrative password, nor any other known password. Further, the rainbow tables that are 99.9% effective were unsuccessful, despite running for days, testing all combinations and tablesets. It is also notable that the FBI has not provided that password, despite numerous requests.[117]

Brad had administrative access to his computer, so he did not need the Administrator password, and according to Cisco, he would not have known the password. There is no innocent reason for the Administrator password to have been reset. It appears that password cracking[118] occurred, which is a clear sign of tampering. Password cracking is an attempt to compromise the user's password so the perpetrator can log on as that user. There are a variety of simple ways to do this, and even an online search will provide "how to" instructions.

The password was suspiciously omitted from the FBI's report on Brad's computer. Officer Chappell testified that identifying and noting the password was "irrelevant" but had to admit that he did include the password in his reports on other computers analyzed in this case. Both

Agents knew it was missing and that it was a major sign of tampering. Their failure to note this was deceptive.

2) Altered Files

On 7/16/08, after Brad had been out of the home for 24 hours, 692 files were *modified*, 251 files were *deleted and created*, and 70 files were *newly created*. Files were also changed on 7/28/08, which is the date the FBI took custody of the computer. <u>The internet history file that allegedly included the Google Maps search was also modified at this time.</u> State experts, Officer Chappell and Special Agent Johnson were unable to specify how they ruled out tampering for each of the 692 files. Again, this is deceptive because the mere fact that the files were changed indicates spoliation occurred. Once that happens, the evidence is no longer reliable.

3) Date and Time

The time and date were last edited on July 15, after the computer was in police custody.

4) Login Attempts

There were three invalid login attempts on the Administrator account. The last one included three successive attempts at 3:10 p.m. on July 15th, and during that exact time, Brad Cooper was on his computer researching the law firm Kurtz & Blum. The login attempts do not show up in the event logs. This is a sign of someone else trying to log into the computer. This may be when the password was cracked.

5) Unexpected Shutdown

The system experienced an unexpected shut down and reboot while Brad was out of the house on July 12, 2008. This was followed by an Administrator login change. Under Cisco's beta testing group, the bracoope account cannot be shut down without manual input. The system either requires a forced reboot or a password to restart the computer. It will not restart itself even for updates. The last event logged through the Windows System 32 Event Logging Application is not on Tuesday July 15 or Wednesday July 16 but occurred Saturday July 12, 2008, at 13:43:53, immediately after this forced, unexpected reboot. This is evidence of a time change.

Jay Ward's Opinion[119]

It is my professional and expert opinion that the IBM ThinkPad was on a network environment within the Cooper residence that was poorly or completely insecure. The posture of this network and the machines that utilized its capabilities for internet service directly resulted in its being vulnerable to a variety of attacks from even the most novice of hackers. Furthermore, per the timeline that I was provided with, it was immediately obvious, upon investigation, that system data had been irrevocably altered after it was confiscated for evidence from Brad Cooper's control and in the sole custody of the Cary Police Department. The nature and extent of the alteration is, for all intents and purposes, impossible to ascertain. There are affirmative indicia of tampering apparent within the dataset. It is my professional opinion and ultimate conclusion that the vulnerabilities of the machine's Operating System, the associated insecure network and coupled with the obviously altered data render the State's forensic examiners' opinions forensically unsound.

231

So, up to this point, we have evidence that was improperly collected, improperly stored, broken chain of custody, multiple file changes, password changes, a time change and invalid login attempts, but we are still supposed to trust the evidence. It's time to take a closer look at the actual Google map files.

The alleged Google Map search took just 42 seconds from the moment Internet Explorer was opened to the moment it closed. In those 42 seconds, maps.google.com is typed into Internet Explorer. When the screen first comes up, it's in the map version, but then it's switched to satellite. That means you can see the terrain and the streets instead of just the streets. It also means that for every page, it has to load two different maps. It starts out as a full map of the United States before "27518" is typed into the Google search box. From that point, the search **makes a direct beeline** to the area over Fielding Drive. There are six separate times when the mouse is clicked to zoom in further. At each zoom level you have to wait until every tile on the screen populates which takes approximately five to six seconds per level. At the exact spot where the body is found, it sits for two seconds, and then the browser closes. There is no wandering, no hesitation.

First View

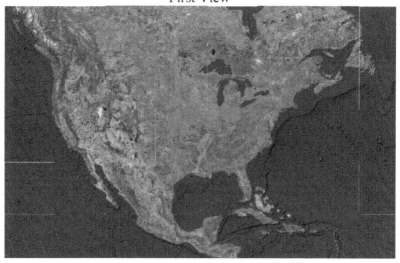

Second View

Third View

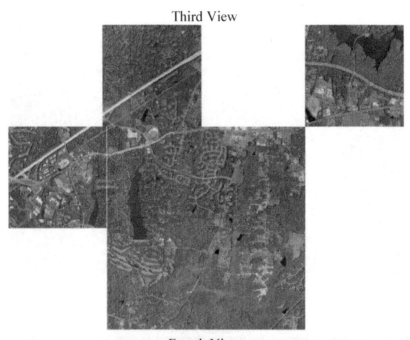

Fourth View

Fifth View

Final View

Consider the logic of the search. Brad allegedly did the search while at the Cisco office. The office has computer labs housed all throughout the campus, and one could easily do an incriminating search on any one of them, but instead, he decides to search for a place to discard a body on his own laptop. Everyone's aware that Google map images are never up to date, and in fact the actual image on the computer was from June 2007—over a year prior to Nancy's death – so it wasn't even an accurate representation of the location. When viewing the final image, one can't even see the main roads that lead to Fielding Drive. How would Brad even know how to get to this location from his home without seeing the main road and without knowing where to turn?

The beeline itself is a strong indication that the files had to have been planted on the machine, as it is not logical for someone searching Google maps for a location to dump a body would do so in a direct line and do no scrolling around. It turns out that there were several anomalies associated with the map files that could not be explained away.

The Missing Cookie

A single item that could have proven whether Brad had Googled the map on that day was a Google cookie. State forensic expert Officer Chappell stated that they found the cookie that matches up with this map search, but they did not.

> "In fact, we have an index.dat history file the week of 7/11 that corroborates the visit to maps.google.com and a cookie for the visit."[120]

During cross-examination he had to admit that his report was incorrect – there was no cookie matching up to the Google map search. No cookie, no deleted cookie.

Officer Chappell's Testimony, Brad Cooper Trial

Q. That's not the question I'm asking. The question is, is there a cookie that exists on the machine that you looked at, that existed on July 11th and was either modified on July 11th or has a modification date that would have included July 11th?

A. Nothing in allocated or recovered deleted, no, sir.

Q. And so the answer is, there's not a single cookie on the machine that corresponds to that visit?

A. Not that we can see from this side, no, sir.

There was no cookie that matched up with the map search, but there are plenty of other cookies on Brad's machine. He had cookies on his machine from the time he acquired it in April and all the way up through July 15. Not one of them is a Google cookie from July 11th. This is significant because it is impossible to fabricate a cookie. Google would know it was **fake**. There's no Google cookie for the map search because it wouldn't have pointed back to Brad.

Although there was no cookie matching up to the search, investigators could have used subsequent Google cookies to verify a prior Google search, and the map search should have been present if it occurred on that machine. Investigators' failure to note this as a clear sign of tampering was deceptive.

Jay Ward's Report

There were seven Google cookies found on the machine. Not one of them matches in date and time to the maps.google.com search on the 11th. They are Google [1], [2], [3], [5], [6], [7], and [8]. There is no corresponding Google cookie. There are no deleted cookies in the

$MFT that would correspond to this Google search. There is no evidence that Mr. Cooper has ever worked to erase history on his ma- machine. There is no evidence of running an erasing program like DBan on the machine. Mr. Cooper clearly did not delete cookies or internet history, as is evidenced by files dating back to April, when the OS was installed. He would not have deleted the matching cookie, especially without taking the easier step of erasing all internet data. And despite checking the other machines for cookies in their report, the FBI did not mention cookies on the ThinkPad.

Private Browsing

Some have suggested that private browsing could have been used. With private browsing, both cookies and temporary internet files are automatically deleted when the browser is closed. There is no evidence that Brad ever used private browsing, and even if he did, the temporary internet files were present but the cookie was missing, so that would not make sense. There is no logical reason for Brad to have gone in and deleted the cookie but left the TIF image files. As well, Agent Johnson testified that private browsing was not utilized, and he also testified that there was no sign of a deleted cookie, and he checked for that. *The only explanation for the missing cookie is that the files did not originate from an organic search.*

Deleted Watermark

Giovanni Masucci uncovered a deleted Google watermark. He testi- fied (for appeal purposes only, not before the jury) that watermarks are proprietary information and that an altered watermark indicates that files had been tampered with.

No Browser History

Masucci also noticed that there was no browser history that matched up to the Google Maps search. The FBI never mentioned this, and it was not brought up at trial. The absence of the browser history is another indication that the files were planted on the machine. The history should have been present. There is nothing on that machine that verified that the search occurred on that machine. The only thing present was the temporary internet files that clearly were not derived from a normal search.

Invalid Timestamps

Every file associated with the Google map search had an invalid timestamp. Over the lifetime of the computer, 2% of the files had invalid timestamps, and there can be legitimate reasons for an invalid timestamp; however, **100% of the map files in question had invalid timestamps**. Again this should have raised red flags when investigators noticed this anomaly because it can be a sign that files were dropped on the machine. Yet, they did nothing to investigate for signs of tampering.

> The state's expert witness, FBI Agent Johnson, testified:
>
> Q. Special Agent Johnson, you actually got a lot of crazy dates on your version of the master file table, same as we did, didn't you?
>
> A. That's correct.
>
> Q. Dates that were hundreds of years in the future?
>
> A. Correct.

Q. And different things that can cause irrational or invalid dates in that column include *placement of files on a hard drive*, do they not?

A. That is included in – in a possible explanation, yes.[121]

Both computer experts for the defense were barred from testifying about the tampering found on Brad's computer; however, Giovanni Masucci testified outside the presence of the jury to preserve his opinions in the event an appeal becomes necessary. His testimony was consistent with Agent Johnson's—invalid timestamps could be indicative of files being dropped on the machine.

Giovanni Masucci's testimony

Q. Now, between July 10th and 12th, there appears to be some multiple of numbers of files with invalid timestamps, compared to files with valid timestamps. And is that something that you've encountered before? Have you seen that kind of situation where you end up with more invalid than valid?

A. That's more indicative of when a file could be dumped on a system, okay? I found some malware okay? That led me to believe – and some of those malwares had back doors, as I stated in my report. When a computer does not understand a file – let's say if a file was dropped on a system, okay, and – and I'm using that term more in layman's than in technical aspect. When a file is – may have been placed on a system, the computer operating system says, well, I don't recognize these files because, you know, the metadata's been stripped out, okay? We see this when – on cases where hackers have hacked in. There's been intrusions, and they strip out the metadata and they go in

240

and they place the data on the – on the drive, on the operating system. <u>And the operating system says, wait a second, I don't recognize them. I can't give you a valid timestamp. You get an invalid timestamp.</u>

Cursor File Anomalies

Jay Ward and Giovanni Masucci examined the Google map cursor files and both confirmed that the format that Google used for their cursors was a **.cur** file. Oddly, the cursor file from the Google map search was a **.bmp** file. That's like saying an incriminating Word file was found whose file extension was .xls instead of .doc. In fact, Agent Johnson replicated the Google map search on September 15, 2008, and it also resulted in a **.cur** file extension. This was only two months after Nancy's death. Google did not change the format, and they did not use **.bmp** extensions.

Furthermore, all MACE (Modify, Access, Create, Entry Modified) timestamps were equal, down to the millisecond. [122] This is extremely significant because it is impossible to have identical timestamps in a dynamic search. As the sole open hand file on the machine (if it were valid), it would have a creation date prior to the search performed on July 11. The Modification Date and Access Dates would also be updated. When there is movement by the mouse, such as zooming in and panning around, the modification and access times will *always* increase. It is not possible for each timestamp to be exactly the same across the board. There is a program called Timestomp that enables one to alter all four file attributes (MACE) in such a way that forensic tools such as FTK(Forensic Tool Kit) considers them to be legitimate timestamps. [123]

Cursor File Found on Brad's Computer

Filename #1
openhand[1].bmp

Std Info Creation date	Std Info Modification date	Std Info Access date	Std Info Entry date
7/11/2008 17:14:53.891	7/11/2008 17:14:53.891	7/11/2008 17:14:53.891	Invalid timestamp

FN Info Creation date	FN Info Modification date	FN Info Access date	FN Info Entry date
7/11/2008 17:14:53.891	7/11/2008 17:14:53.891	7/11/2008 17:14:53.891	7/11/2008 17:14:53.891

Filename #1
closedhand[1].bmp

Std Info Creation date	Std Info Modification date	Std Info Access date	Std Info Entry date
7/11/2008 17:15:13.601	7/11/2008 17:15:13.601	7/11/2008 17:15:13.601	Invalid timestamp

FN Info Creation date	FN Info Modification date	FN Info Access date	FN Info Entry date
7/11/2008 17:15:13.601	7/11/2008 17:15:13.601	7/11/2008 17:15:13.601	7/11/2008 17:15:13.601

Duplicating the Google Map search

Defense experts ran several test replications to see exactly how the cursor files would appear. Without fail, in every test replication as the page is navigated (whether it's by a mouse, track pad or dial), the cursor time increases. The search that was allegedly done to find Fielding Drive included several levels of zoom. This could not happen without a cursor time change. It is impossible. Yet all seven timestamps (the 8th was invalid) associated with the Google Map files on Brad's computer are the same. <u>They did not increment</u>. This is irrefutable evidence of tampering. The Google open hand and closed hand files were not artifacts of a valid search, but were placed inside the computer to frame Brad Cooper for murder. There is no other valid explanation. What would cause identical timestamps?

Defense Attorney Howard Kurtz questioned Agent Johnson about the significance of identical timestamps.

Q. There is no time reflected as being elapsed from the create time through the access time on either the open hand or closed hand cursor, is that correct?

A. That's correct.

Q. If you were to place files from a hard drive onto another computer, is there a likelihood of all file timestamps being identical?

A. I understand you're taking from one hard drive to another.

Q. Correct.

A. Okay, and you want to know about the –

Q. At that time that they're manipulated, is it possible that all file timestamps, at that point, reset when moved from point A to point B?

A. They – <u>it is possible for them to reset</u>.

Q. Is it also possible that there are programs that would allow you to predetermine a time for all – for all of the timestamps to reflect, if you were to move things from one drive to another?

A. I'm not familiar with any such programs but it would be possible to do that, yes.

Q. And is it possible that moving files from one drive to another could result in an invalid timestamp in the system information attribute entry modified column, in specific?

A. It could.

What does this mean?

If one were to do a particular Google map search on one computer and wanted to transfer the files onto another computer to make it appear that it originated there, they would have to change the time on the file. The time on the cursor file was approximately 1:14 p.m., July 11, 2008. However, it appears that when the files were placed on the machine it caused the timestamps to "reset," making them all appear to be identical and also rendering every single file (over 500) associated with the search invalid. This wasn't a seamless hack. The evidence of tampering is visible to those who know what to look for.

Although the prosecution's own witness testified that invalid and identical timestamps can result from files being placed on a machine, he made no effort to rule out tampering. This *was* evidence of tampering. Was this a competent investigation? It is clear that the State made no effort to investigate the tampering claims. Their case depended on the computer evidence. They knew they couldn't win without it, so they proceeded as if the evidence was reliable. They should have hired someone like defense expert Jay Ward to investigate for tampering. Jay Ward specializes in identifying signs of intrusions. The State forensic experts simply carved out the data with forensic tools. They did not routinely investigate for tampering. Ward testified about all the steps required to conduct a thorough assessment. The State experts did not do these things.

The State experts did not do a penetration assessment. They did not request router logs, did not red flag anomalies such as invalid timestamps, attempted logins and malware. They did not red flag the fact that files were changed while the computer was in police custody. They made no effort to identify what happened with the files. They did not even preserve the evidence through Google. Further, they misstated facts in their tampering report—stated that there was a cookie when there was not; stated that there may have been MAC filtering knowing there was not. According to Agent Johnson's report, there was no confidence in the validity of the map files. It states, "*Appears to have been created,*" when all other activities use affirmative and secure language. [124]

Although Agent Johnson examined and wrote the report on his findings, he did not testify about the Google map search files. This was peculiar. Was he worried about being associated with planted evidence? Officer Chappell testified about the map files, but was he actually involved in the examination of that computer? That is unclear, but his testimony indicated he did not have much knowledge about the evidence. For example, he didn't stitch together the tiles to determine how the search would have occurred. He didn't determine the amount of time at each zoom level or whether or not the browser closed after the search. Brad's expert did all of that and determined exactly how it would have occurred.

If things were reversed and the government accused a person of hacking into a system and went to court and presented the tampering evidence found on Brad's computer, the hacker would be convicted. There is no doubt. All the signs were there—evidence of penetration, administrator account changes, malware, no recoverable password, broken chain of custody, invalid Google map files and the absence of a cookie. Since the hacking claim was made against the police, nothing was done about it. The judge allowed the prosecution to press forward and present the invalid map files as if they were authentic (they were not).

Who planted the files?

It's impossible to know who planted the files on Brad's computer, but there is very strong reason to believe that police and prosecutors knew that the files weren't authentic.

❖ They intentionally allowed the privacy policy to lapse, making it impossible for anyone to ever verify the IP address of the search with Google.

❖ It was the most important evidence. They should have wanted proof that Brad did the search; instead they intentionally avoided all possible avenues to procure that irrefutable evidence.

❖ They put up road blocks so that the defense would not receive full discovery – hid behind the FBI and used national security as reasons to deny the defense request.

❖ They delayed supplying the defense with a copy of the hard drive for six months for no reason.

❖ They fought at trial to prevent their own expert from duplicating the map search in court.

❖ They found creative ways to convince the judge that no defense expert should be permitted to testify about the tampering evidence.

The files could have been planted by police, the FBI or both, or they could have been planted by one of the suspicious alternate suspects who were never investigated, possibly John Pearson or the Adams. Or maybe it was done by the investigators working with the law firm used by Nancy's parents in the custody case. The firm wouldn't necessarily have had to even know about it, but their investigators were running surveillance on Brad and following him and were definitely involved in the case from the beginning. This is all speculation, because no steps were ever taken by investigators or the DA's office to explore the allegations of tampering or to attempt to identify those who may have been responsible for the framing of Brad Cooper, but the evidence can't be denied.

It's difficult for some people to fathom that public officials could allow something like this to happen, or further, that they may have even been directly involved in the framing of Brad Cooper. Instead, they go on believing that Brad did the Google Map search, despite the obvious signs of tampering. The reality is that it is easy to hack into a computer and change files. Anyone who knows anything about computers understands that. That is the sole reason that stringent procedures for handling digital evidence must be followed if it is to have any reliability. The egregious actions of every official who had a hand in this can't be overstated.

- Police mishandled the evidence.
- FBI agents failed to authenticate the evidence and then failed to investigate for signs of tampering.
- Prosecutors delayed sharing the evidence – purposely allowing a critical deadline to expire and then abused their power by using national security to avoid sharing discovery.
- Judge Gessner accepted the unreliable evidence, knowing full well that it could not be trusted.

Every one of them had the power to prevent false evidence from convicting a person but instead chose to go along with the charade. It is inexcusable, but the government can abuse their authority to trample all over citizens' rights, and they are rarely held accountable.

{ 20 }

Interesting Facts about the Computer Evidence

1. Forensic Preview

In a December 2008 search warrant, Detective Young referenced a forensic preview on Brad's computer at a time when the computer would have still been in the custody of Cary Police and the hard drive had not yet been hashed, thus leaving it vulnerable to tampering. This is the same cop who attempted to do a forensic preview of Nancy's phone and then permanently deleted all data. There is no mention of the forensic preview in FBI Agent Johnson's report and no mention that protocols had been breached. Detective Young testified that he did not do a forensic preview on Brad's computer and is unaware of anyone having done one. So why is it stated in a search warrant?

> "In addition, the forensics preview of the IBM ThinkPad laptop computer indicated that Brad Cooper read e-mails sent to. . . ."

(Cary Police search warrant, December 2008)

2. Robert Petrick Case:

It is an interesting coincidence that there happened to be another local case where Google searches were allegedly used to find a location to dump a body. There are no other instances of this anywhere in the country aside from this one other case in neighboring Durham County. Robert Petrick was convicted of murdering his wife Janine Sutphen in 2005. In the middle of the trial, the State found evidence on his computer – searches for water conditions at Falls Lake – the location where the body would later be found. Petrick also worked in the IT field as a computer consultant. Officer Chappell was with the Durham Police Department, the same department that investigated the Petrick case. Is it possible that the Petrick case inspired those who framed Brad Cooper?

> "In a murder trial featuring evidence of Google searches, jurors late Tuesday found former computer consultant Robert Petrick guilty of first degree murder in the killing of his wife.
> Petrick, who represented himself during the North Carolina trial, is expected to appeal and has requested a court-appointed lawyer. Jurors rejected Petrick's attempts to convince them that *Google searches* for the words 'neck,' 'snap,' 'break,' and 'hold' uncovered on his hard drive were done by another user." [125]

3. Unusual Wording

"At 1:14 p.m. Brad conducts a Google map search of Fielding Drive and enhances the satellite view to show the exact location of where Nancy's body was later recovered. The amount of time Brad spends looking at the Google map is 45 seconds. This information was con-firmed through a forensic investigation of Brad's laptop computer which was conducted by the FBI." [126]

Note: If the FBI "discovered" the map search, it is odd that Cary Police referenced that it was *confirmed* by the FBI, as if it was already known that it existed and the FBI was simply confirming it.

4. 178 Greenstone Lane

Bate	Person	Description
00480		➢ July 11 13:14:53 Google search ➢ July 11 13:14:59 Google search for 178 Greenstone Lane
00522		➢ July 11 13:14:53 Open Google ➢ July 11 13:14:59 search for 27518

This address, which was listed in the Cary Police Department's reports does not exist, but if it did, it is very close to the zip code coordinates 27518—which they allege was first typed into Google maps. Was this address used in the framing of Brad Cooper? Detective Daniels denied having any knowledge of it when questioned about it at trial. Officer Chappell also testified that he had no knowledge of it. Someone had to know something about this, as it was included in discovery.

The two sets of coordinates were compared in Google Maps, searching with zip code 27518 and then 178 Greenstone Lane. The images are very close. The significance of this non-existent address remains a mystery.

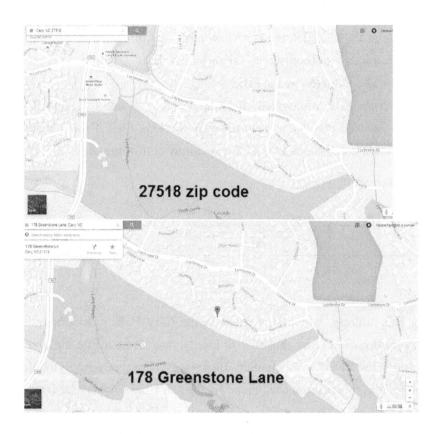

27518 zip code

178 Greenstone Lane

5. Map Search Not Referenced

Though it is common practice for police to reference their strongest evidence in search warrants, the map search was omitted from all warrants in this case. Cary Police learned of the search on September 5, 2008. They had dozens of search warrants. Each one contains a probable cause section with justification for why the search or order is necessary. Trivial information was included but not the map search. What possible reason would Cary Police have for omitting this information? One reason why it may not have been included is because a police officer has to swear to the authenticity and accuracy of facts. If they sign a search warrant that knowingly contains false information, they are committing perjury. Another reason they may have withheld it is that it would have given Brad's attorneys the awareness and thus the opportunity to verify whether or not the search originated on Brad's computer.

Cary Police actually investigated another murder case earlier in 2008 —the death of Vanlata Patel. The search warrant for the defendant's computer contained very similar wording as the warrant in the Cooper case except for one phrase—files indicating travel, *including maps*. Oddly, the Cooper search warrant made no mention of maps.

Patel Search Warrant: In seeking the warrant, investigators said they would examine the contents of directories and files and perform keyword searches for evidence linking the computer to the death of Vanlata Patel. Specifically, the warrant listed —

* ❖ Financial documents and financial inquires
* ❖ Files relating to news coverage of the death of Vanlata Patel
* ❖ Files relating to methods of committing murder
* ❖ Files relating to methods of disposing of a body
* ❖ Files indicating travel, <u>including maps</u>[127]

As mentioned, the Cooper search warrant made *no mention of maps.*

* ❖ Any and all temporary Internet files or other digital history files indicating computer and/or Internet usage.
* ❖ Any and all file (word documents, video clips, audio files, audio recordings, image files, e-mails and other digital files), to include any and all file attachments related to the

homicide of Nancy Lynn Cooper and/or illustrate and/or provide evidence of the marital discord of Bradley and Nancy Cooper.

- ❖ Financial documents and other documents indicating financial inquiries, withdrawals or other transactions which illustrate and/or provide evidence of the marital discord of Bradley and Nancy Cooper.
- ❖ Files relating to instructions, methods or means of committing the crime of homicide.
- ❖ Files relating to instructions, methods of committing the crime of homicide.
- ❖ Files relating to instructions, methods or means of disposing of a human body.

Equally as odd, prosecutors did not mention the Google search in opening arguments, even though it is standard to describe the most compelling evidence with the jury. They also saved the map evidence for last. This is an indication that they didn't have confidence in the evidence. Perhaps they even contemplated excluding it from the trial altogether. Once they realized how poorly their case was going, they had to use it. Once they realized that they had to use it, they were compelled to block Brad's defense experts from testifying. Luckily for them, they had a judge willing to go along with the railroading, even with the knowledge that his rulings would likely result in the conviction being overturned.

{ 21 }

Circumventing Discovery Via National Security

The Brady Rule, named for Brady v. Maryland373 U.S. 83 (1963), requires prosecutors to disclose materially exculpatory evidence in the government's possession to the defense. "Brady material" or evidence the prosecutor is required to disclose under this rule includes any evidence favorable to the accused - evidence that goes towards negating a defendant's guilt, that would reduce a defendant's potential sentence, or evidence going to the credibility of a witness.[128]

Seven months before Brad's trial, prosecutors presented the court with an affidavit[129] from an FBI agent (FBI Agent Durie) asserting that the defense should not be entitled to discovery materials pertaining to the computer evidence because the FBI performed the analysis. It sought to exclude the investigators' bench notes, procedures, extraction methods and all of the underlying data used to form their opinion about the evidence found on Brad's computer. It further stated that sharing any of this information could potentially jeopardize the national security of the United States. This was outrageous. This was evidence obtained from Brad's computer. There were no national security issues. Clearly they didn't want the defense to have an opportunity to scrutinize the unreliable FBI data, so they used national security as a shield. There are terrorism cases where national security is touted as a reason for not turning over files, but there are ways to keep things transparent for both parties without making the infor-

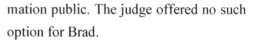

mation public. The judge offered no such option for Brad.

Basically, the government said, "We found incriminating evidence on your computer but we can't show it to you because it's a secret." This put the defense at a huge disadvantage because it impeded their ability to show the jury the flaws and insufficiencies in the FBI's conclusions. Normally the defense team can scrutinize the State's evidence and sometimes can completely refute it by simply noticing errors or inaccurate conclusions. This alone could have been enough to prove Brad's innocence, but nothing was shared. The Judge ruled in favor of the State to withhold this important discovery from Brad.

Since the State wouldn't even share the tool used in the extraction of the hard drive, the defense expert had to work with blinders on, not knowing if his data and the FBI's data would match identically. Different tools can yield slightly different data. This meant that Brad's attorneys couldn't question the state witnesses about the master file table from the hard drive because he would be referencing a different set of data. The master file table is one of the main things the forensic examiner will look at to analyze the computer activity.

> The NTFS file system contains a file called the *master file table*, or MFT. There is at least one entry in the MFT for every file on an NTFS file system volume, including the MFT itself. <u>All information about a file, including its size, time and date stamps, permissions, and data content, is stored either in MFT entries, or in space outside the MFT that is described by MFT entries.</u>[130]

Brad's attorney Howard Kurtz had to beg the court for a copy of the FBI's master file table and finally received it in the middle of the trial. He had to fight against the prosecution throughout the trial as issues continued to arise related to the blocked computer evidence. ADA Boz Zellinger mischaracterized the magnitude of the withheld discovery evidence multiple times by claiming that the defense had all the evidence because they had a copy of the hard drive. The claim was deceptive and false because there are thousands of logs and files contained on a hard drive. It is the *data* from the drive that's important, not the drive itself!

None of this would have been possible if Cary Police had used anyone other than the FBI to do the analysis. They were only able to play the "national security" card because it was the FBI. They could have used a private examiner or the SBI. They had many options that would have kept things fair. This issue was the largest contributor to the unfairness of the trial. The implications are frightening because it means that anytime the government wants to convict a person with shaky evidence, they can hire the FBI to do the testing and then say that national security prohibits the defense from receiving discovery. It was an enormous violation of Brad's rights.

Why the FBI?

Detective Josh Bonin of the Cary Police had been assigned to the FBI Cybercrime task force and testified that the agents offered their assistance when they learned about the case. The agent who subsequently became involved in the case (Agent Johnson) testified that Bonin approached *him* about their potential assistance in the investigation.

"While I was assigned to the FBI as a Task Force Agent with Cyber Crimes Unit, I learned about a homicide that occurred in Cary via the news. While discussing the news release with several agents, it was brought up that the FBI would be willing to assist the CPD if needed." (Officer Bonin, Cary Police)

"After being instructed to contact one of the detectives with the CPD working with the case, and extend an offer of assistance, I made contact with Detective Jim Young. I informed Detective Young that the FBI would be willing to assist if needed. A short time after I spoke with Detective Young, he contacted me by telephone and said they could use some assistance with parts of the technical aspects of the investigation. I then put Detective Young in contact with Special Agent Gregory Johnson and Task Force Agent Christopher Chappell." (Officer Bonin 7/24/08 CPD narrative #163) [131]

258

A scandal broke out in April, 2015 that described the FBI's history of misreporting evidence in thousands of cases.

> "Nearly every examiner in an elite FBI forensic unit gave flawed testimony in almost all trials in which they offered evidence against criminal defendants over more than a two-decade period before 2000," the newspaper reported, adding that "the cases include those of 32 defendants sentenced to death." The article notes that the admissions from the FBI and Department of Justice "confirm long-suspected problems with subjective, pattern-based forensic techniques—like hair and bite-mark comparisons—that have contributed to wrongful convictions in more than one-quarter of 329 DNA-exoneration cases since 1989."[132]

If there are such extensive instances of flawed testimony with other types of FBI evidence, why not computer evidence too?

{ 22 }

Judge Completely Blocks Defense Case

Judge Paul Gessner

It's already been established that there were multiple problems with the way the computer evidence was handled. It was improperly collected and stored, there were chain of custody issues, it was not third party verified, and when the defense finally analyzed the hard drive, there were multiple signs of intrusion. The computer evidence should have been inadmissible, but the judge accepted it. This was very disturbing and should be of great concern to everyone because it was a blatant violation of the judicial process. Imagine being convicted of a crime based on tainted evidence!

Beginning long before the trial in a very systematic fashion, the State began blocking all avenues for the defense to counter this very questionable computer evidence. It began when they delayed giving the defense a copy of the hard drive until it was impossible to confirm the search through Google, then they cited national security concerns to withhold discovery, and the blocking continued into the trial.

The defense gave the State a copy of computer expert Jay Ward's report as part of mutual discovery requirements. The report summarized his opinion that tampering had occurred on Brad's computer. In the middle of the trial, prosecutors filed a motion to receive the underlying data used by Ward to form his opinion. The judge ordered the defense to provide the data. Consider now that Brad wasn't allowed to see any of the FBI's underlying data, but the State was granted all of the defense expert's data. Is that fair? "We don't have to share because we're the FBI"?!

Nonetheless, the prosecution received all of Ward's data. Shockingly, after they received it, they moved to block him from testifying about his conclusions. The prosecution knew long before trial that the defense planned to call Jay Ward to testify as an expert, but they did not alert the defense that there were any issues. This would have given the defense time to arrange a back-up expert. Side note—in a criminal trial, a witness must be deemed an expert by the court in order to offer their *opinions* about the matter. If they are not considered qualified as an "expert" they can still testify but can't say, "It is my opinion that tampering occurred."

They waited until the trial began, and after a voir dire (qualification testimony outside the jury's presence), they argued that Ward should not be permitted to testify as an expert because he was not qualified to do forensic examinations as he had only done a few throughout his career. However, there was never any intent for Ward to testify as a "forensic" examiner. He is not a forensic examiner. He is a network security expert. Forensic examiners carve data from machines and analyze the contents. Brad needed Ward's expertise in identifying signs of tampering because he did not do what the State was accusing him of. He did not do a Google Map search of Fielding Drive and he needed to prove it through this expert's knowledge.

It was improper for the State to object to Ward testifying as an expert because he analyzes hard drives routinely as part of his responsibilities securing company networks against intrusions. The defense case depended on the ability to show the jury the clear signs of tampering that were found on Brad's computer. Nonetheless, the judge sided with the State and would only permit him to testify as a "network security" expert. This meant that he would not be permitted to testify about any *specific* signs of intrusion on Brad's machine, any signs of tampering or any specific problems with the actual files. Ward did testify, but the limited context of his testimony didn't offer what was necessary for Brad to prove he was framed.

The prosecution succeeded in blocking testimony from Brad's defense expert and they couldn't have done it without Judge Gessner. He played a role in the railroading, but the unethical tactics didn't stop there. When Ward was cross-examined, ADA Boz Zellinger attempted to attack and discredit him by bringing up various things from his Facebook page. For example, he tried to suggest that Ward wasn't capable of securing his Facebook privacy settings because his page was publicly viewable – implying that he was negligent with his Facebook settings. Of course, one is free to maintain their Facebook page at any security level they wish, but the judge allowed this line of questioning. It was a disgusting display.

Duplication of the Map Search

Remember that the defense experts had duplicated the map search and found that the cursor files incremented in every test case performed. State expert, Agent Chappell testified that he too duplicated the map search. He visited the Google map site and manipulated the map to move to the center in an attempt to replicate the files found on Brad's computer. The examiners offered their opinion that the files on Brad's laptop were created by someone using that computer when it was at the Cisco offices at 1:14 p.m. on July 11, 2008, to do a map search for the zip code 27518 and then moving east on the map and zooming in until the image was centered over the area where Nancy's body was found. The defense only learned of this experiment during Chappell's testimony. They were given no reports or conclusions prior to trial.[133] Having this information before trial would have allowed the defense the ability to prepare to question him. As well, they should have received a copy of the results, but nothing about this case was fair. This was another Brady violation.

Defense Calls Agent Johnson

The defense wasn't willing to give up. They had proof that Brad was framed with the Google map files and they needed to find a way to get it before the jury. During voir dire (outside the presence of the jury), Agent Johnson testified that he still had the test data from the duplication of the Google Map search described by Officer Chappell. In fact there is a screenshot of the cursor files in the discovery, but *only the first column is visible*. This was potentially crucial evidence to support the defense claim that the Google Map files were planted. If the timestamps in the cursor files from the Google Map experiment changed as the cursor was moved, it would conclusively prove that the Google map files on Brad's computer were the product of tampering.

Asserting that a test of how Google Maps functions could have no ramifications to national security, the defense requested to view a copy of that data. Judge Gessner denied the motion, citing that it was covered by the national security protected privilege. He further ruled that the defense would not be allowed to question Agent Johnson about whether or why any national security issue would be created if that data was produced. The data was not produced.[134] **This was wrong**. This was not a request for FBI secret methods. It was a simple request for a copy of the cursor files generated from the FBI's test. It did not fall under the national security umbrella at all, but they simply couldn't allow the defense to *prove* that the map files were placed on the machine.

At that point, defense attorney Howard Kurtz asked Agent Johnson if he would duplicate the search right then and there. He had a computer with a Windows Vista operating system so that everything would be the same as Brad's computer at the time of the alleged search. The State objected. The jury was sent out again. The prosecutor argued that it wasn't a controlled environment, Johnson could only do this in a lab, and he didn't know the history of the computer the defense offered. Kurtz offered that any computer in the courtroom could be used. The judge refused to allow it. **Every effort to reveal the truth was thwarted**, first by barring the defense expert from testifying and then by claiming that the country would be in danger if the FBI agent showed them a document! This infringed upon Brad's basic right to confront his accuser. This was a pivotal part of the trial because it basically sealed Brad's fate. The jury would never get to see proof that the tampering claims were legitimate.

<u>The following is part of the defense voir dire (outside the presence of jury) questioning of Agent Johnson</u>:

Kurtz: Do you still have the test data?

Johnson: I'm sure we do. I believe that was a large part of Officer Chappell's testimony.

Kurtz: The test data that resulted from Officer Chappell and your testing, is that particular data in any way a jeopardy to national security if it was disclosed to us?

ADA Zellinger: Your Honor, I'm going to object. This is far outside the scope of determining whether that computer is proper for an examination. And we're also delving into an issue of law here for the Court and not for Agent Johnson.

Kurtz: Well, Judge, there is potentially a piece of information that exists on Mr. Cooper's computer that could say definitely that this material was planted, absolutely definitive. I may be wrong. Special Agent Johnson's testing may indeed be that it all has the exact same millisecond all the way across. I don't think I'm wrong.

Now, one way or the other, whether it's having a test done on a Vista machine now and seeing what it – what it actually **shows or giving us access to the original test data, which I don't believe has any national security ramifications since it** deals with a Google map test. One way or the other, we should be entitled to this information as it could be tremendously exculpatory.

The Court: Upon reconsidering this issue about this in-court test, pursuant to Rule 403, I'm going to sustain the objection and exclude any testing in Court because of the differences in the equipment and the statements made by this witness that this is not the appropriate place to do it. We need to bring the jury back in. And regarding the **national security issue**, that is a matter that we have already ruled on. It is something I have already dealt with.

Kurtz: But, Your Honor, there is a witness on the stand that can answer specifically whether this is an issue of national security. And I'm not even going to be allowed to ask that question?

The Court: I believe I've already determined, because of the rules of the – and the discovery process that you are not entitled to get those things.

Kurtz: So my understanding is, the rules and the discovery process, we're hiding behind national security on an issue where we could get a clear answer from a witness that this is not in fact a national security issue. And we're talking about a piece of information that could be exculpatory to Mr. Cooper.

ADA Zellinger: Your Honor, first of all, the exculpatory information is already in the Defendant's possession. He has all the files. The fact that his expert is – his expert can't speak to that is what the issue is before the Court. But as to any exculpatory information, all that has been given to the defendant. All those computer files have been given to the Defendant. So I want to just take issue with that and I just wanted to put that on the record, as to the rest regarding –

Kurtz: Your Honor, that is an inaccurate statement because we're not talking about data from this computer. We're talking about data that Special Agent Johnson and Officer Chappell generated when they attempted to replicate the search. When they replicated this search, they will have generated – and in fact, we've got a screen shot that shows the first of the timestamps. There are additional timestamps that are off screen. Those additional timestamps would answer this question definitely. And there can be no national security issue here, given we're talking about Mr. Cooper's computer alone and the data that was generated during their testing.

The Court: It's the methodology that they used, I think, that falls under the security issue but –

Kurtz: But if I could ask Special Agent Johnson if he has any national security concerns related to that methodology, we might be able to determine that this one particular test is a legitimate one to be disclosed, that it will not actually disclose the missile codes.

ADA Zellinger: Your Honor, I'm looking at the affidavit of the FBI agent who provided an affidavit to the Court on June 10th of 2010. And that set out the FBI current policies and procedures for the viewing, extraction, and or examination of digital data, the FBI's policies on the analysis, or – or how it was – how it was examined, numerous other documents from FBI Special Agent Johnson pertaining to his examination of the computers in this case, including but not limited to, communication logs, examiner bench notes, and all other documents completed or compiled by Special Agent Johnson beyond the report of the examination. That's what we're seeking to protect here, because we don't want, pursuant to state case law, we – the standard operating procedures of the FBI are protected throughout our nation. And we're not hiding behind anything. All that information's been given to the Defendant. Agent Johnson's given out more information in this case than he's ever given out in any other case. And as to the – specific material that the Defendant wants, he has these files. If – if they're exculpatory, take them to an expert and find out how they're exculpatory.

But the fact is that these files the Defendant has in his possession. Asking Agent Johnson on voir dire about national security just seems wildly inappropriate to me, and then he wants to know exactly how every part of every test that Agent Johnson does can affect national security and that people could be put in danger or child pornography could – could easily be deleted after this information comes out. And we're re-litigating this issue again.

Kurtz: Your Honor, what Mr. Zellinger is saying is flat out dishonest and is ascertainable by asking Special Agent Johnson if this is information that we ever got. He's saying we have these files; we don't have these files. These are not the files from Mr. Cooper's computer. These are files from Special Agent Johnson and Chappell's tests.

The Court: The objection is sustained. I'm not going to allow further questioning in this line or any in-court testing of that computer. We need to bring in the jury.

Kurtz: Your Honor, at this time I am moving for a mistrial and asking your Honor to recuse. I believe that your bias throughout this trial has become apparent. I am making this motion pursuant to the Fifth and Sixth Amendments to the U.S. Constitution, the Fourteenth Amendment of the U.S. Constitution, North Carolina State Constitution, Sections 19 and 23. I believe that your rulings have consistently been outside the bounds of prudent jurisprudence.

The Court: Your objection and motion is noted for the record. Your motion is denied.

Mr. Kurtz: And as to this particular issue, my inability to get exculpatory information from Special Agent Johnson's testing, I am also Constitutionalizing that objection pursuant to the Fifth and Sixth

Amendments to the United States Constitution, along with the Fourteenth and Sections 19 and 23, Article One of the North Carolina State Constitution.

The Court: They are noted for the record and overruled. If you'll bring in the jury.

After this, direct questioning continued, but imagine what Brad must have been thinking when all of this was happening—the only thing standing in the way of an acquittal, absolute proof that he was framed with the Google Map files, was concealed at all costs with the judge and prosecutors knowing full well that what they were doing was unlawful and that these actions would likely result in the conviction being reversed. ADA Zellinger was absolutely deceiving the judge when he continued to claim that the defense had all the evidence. They had Brad's hard drive and that was it. They were requesting data from when the FBI duplicated the Google Map search on a different computer to see how the files appeared.

The whole purpose of a trial is to have all the evidence before the jury so that they can make an informed decision about the person's guilt or innocence. That didn't happen in this case. An honest prosecutor would have wanted to hear about the results of the test and would have allowed them to be shared in court, but Zellinger chose to block the evidence. An honest judge would have supported the defense request to view the results of the experiment. He refused. They wanted to win and did not care about the truth.

One Final Hope

The defense had one final hope in getting the crucial evidence before the jury. A forensic examiner, Giovanni Masucci, came forward and volunteered to assist the defense. Masucci examined and compared Jay Ward's data with the FBI's data and found that the master file tables contained an identical number of files. It confirmed Ward's methods were sound. He therefore concurred with his findings and endorsed all of the conclusions reached by Ward. He reported his conclusion that the Google map files in the temporary internet folders on Brad's computer were not created as the result of an organic and genuine internet search from that computer, that they were files placed on the computer from another source. [135]

Masucci was fully prepared to testify, but this was also blocked. The prosecutors said that Masucci should not be permitted to testify because he wasn't on the original witness list, and additionally, they did not have enough time to prepare to cross-examine him. They shouldn't have needed any additional time to prepare if in fact they were already prepared to question Ward because their findings were consistent. However, it was no surprise that the judge sided with the State. This ruling was improper, but by that point it was no surprise. Brad's final hope was shot down. It was a devastating blow to his case.

The judge didn't even attempt to conceal his bias. The prosecution's case was based on hearsay from the neighbors and presentation of a bunch of irrelevant evidence that did not in any way indicate Brad's guilt. The meaningless testimony from the State was allowed; the defense testimony pertaining to the only evidence linking Brad to Nancy's death was blocked. It is shocking that this could happen, and yet this judge is still running unopposed every election and remains on the bench. *Update 10/18/15* — Days after this book was published, Judge Gessner announced he was stepping down from the bench and going to work with the Wake County Sherriff's Department.

This case is unique in the sense that the tampering claims were launched against public officials who severely mishandled evidence. It is difficult to find a case similar to this. It probably has occurred before, but it's likely that things don't usually go this far, and so we never hear about it. There were many steps along the way where someone could have stepped in and stopped this. Initially, the FBI could have informed the Cary Police that something wasn't right with the computer and that the evidence appeared to be tainted. In an honest investigation, it would have ended there. Cary Police could have admitted that they didn't follow forensic protocols and the evidence couldn't be trusted. Certainly the FBI could have refused to be associated with the case, but they did not. Next, the district attorney's office could have stopped this and investigated the reasons for the failure of the Cary Police and could have also attempted to determine how the files got on Brad's computer, but instead they chose to stall so that the files could never be third-party verified. Then they produced a ridiculous FBI affidavit about national security and blocked Brad's defense case at trial. The judge was next. He certainly had the ultimate authority to stop this. He is the one to decide when evidence should be declared inadmissible, and this evidence certainly met the criteria. No one would have faulted him for rejecting it, but he chose to conduct a sham trial. They all failed, and the result was devastating to Brad Cooper and to everyone who cares about justice and fair trials.

{ 23 }

The Jury

There were a couple of interesting things worth noting about the jury. First, Jessica Adam inserted herself into the case one last time during the trial by contacting the prosecutors to inform them that a juror was gossiping about the case with her hairdresser.

> Karen, Amy, Howard and Boz,
> Wanted to let you know that one of the jurors on the Cooper case is apparently sharing information with a friend. A juror's friend went into a hair salon (my hair salon) yesterday and very loudly discussed details about the case. This woman (Stacy Gallager) recounted her juror friend's statements and concerns that the case is purely circumstantial, how the jury is comprised of mostly stay-at-home housewives and her apparent concern with missing her vacation in May. It alarmed me and I wanted to make sure you knew.
> Many thanks,[136]
> Jessica Adam

Some of the notes sent to the judge were disturbing, particularly the one that stated that they "wanted their lives back." It was written part-way through the defense case. Had the state not dragged out the testimony for seven or so long weeks, the jurors wouldn't have felt so worn out. Did they even listen to the defense case, or had they had enough?

Judge Gessner,

Please encourage the attorneys to use time more wisely. Shortened days prolong this process. We are hoping to finish this soon! Please ask them to have their witnesses ready to go. We want our lives back.

Thank you —

Court's exhibit #8

4-28-11   12:39pm KH

This one is interesting because the verdict was read on May 5th. Was there pressure to speed up deliberations? This is also consistent with Jessica Adam's letter to the prosecution regarding the concern about going into May. Did the prosecution use that information to their advantage?

Court exhibit #11
5-3-11 4:31 pm

Daughter's last exam
May 4, 2011

*Has to be out of
her dorm by
May 5, 2011

picking her up
from Winston Salem

Thanks!

On May 5, 2011 the jury convicted Brad Cooper of first degree murder with a mandatory sentence of life without parole. None of the jurors has ever spoken to the media. They all declined to be interviewed by Dateline or any other news organizations. The only public statement was made by the jury foreman.

"It is my personal belief that we (the jurors) came into this process verdict-neutral. Brad Cooper was innocent until proven guilty," jury foreman Andy Gilbert said in an email this week to WRAL News and other media outlets. "I came into this situation neutral, and I left it that way. The evidence was the only factor in determining our verdict."

Specifically, Gilbert said, was testimony from two FBI agents who testified about Internet searches on Brad Cooper's laptop computer, including maps of the location where his wife's body was found.

"The evidence presented by Special Agents (Gregory) Johnson and (Chris) Chappell drove the outcome on this case," he said. "It caused a lot of the other circumstantial evidence to become relevant and credible."[137]

While it's understandable that the jury found the map evidence incriminating, it was still improper for them to vote Guilty. First, a Guilty vote meant that they believed the 6:40 a.m. phone call was automated. The State didn't meet the burden of proof and did nothing more than present ways Brad "could have" spoofed the call. The jurors must have missed the *facts* that negated the State's claims. The jury is not supposed to convict based on one's *ability* to do something. Proof is required. It is common today for the prosecution to trick juries into believing there is "mountains" of circumstantial evidence when in fact there is nothing but fabricated evidence and speculations. They do not understand that the evidence must be fact based.

Second, the prosecution didn't provide any evidence that Brad did the Google Map search because they failed to take the standard step of third-party verification. Again, the burden of proof was on the State. And third, there was no other evidence linking Brad to Nancy's death in any way. Therefore, Brad should have been acquitted.

A final thought about this jury and others in general: it seems obvious they were worn down and ready to go home. After all, the trial had lasted ten long weeks. Jurors often believe that if they make a mistake it is no big deal—it will be sorted out on appeal. There is a misconception that it is easy to overturn a conviction, but in fact it is almost impossible.

{ 24 }

Appeal

Attorney Ann Petersen was assigned to handle Brad's appeal. The first appeal in a criminal case is always based on improper judicial rulings. The attorney must prove that the judge abused his discretion by ruling improperly and that it is so severe that the verdict can't be trusted. In other words, the impact of the judge's errors must be severe enough that had he ruled properly the jury may have reached a different verdict. Naturally, the most extreme rulings were argued in a brief for the North Carolina Court of Appeal. Though there were dozens of improper rulings, the following three points were argued. The response of the Court of Appeal follows each argument.

I. Precluding the testimony of Giovanni Masucci as a sanction for purported discovery violations was an abuse of discretion and deprived defendant Brad Cooper of his state and federal constitutional due process right to present a defense.

Court's ruling: "In light of the lack of willful misconduct on the part of Defendant, the rational reason presented for failing to inform the State before trial that Defendant would be calling Masucci, the role of the State in having the situation arise after the trial had commenced, the fundamental nature of the rights involved, the importance to the defense of the testimony excluded, and the minimal prejudice to the state had the trial court imposed a lesser sanction – such as continuance or recess, <u>we hold that imposing the harsh sanction of excluding Masucci from testifying constituted an abuse of discretion</u>."

II. The trial court's ruling that Jay Ward was not qualified to give expert testimony about tampering on defendant Brad Cooper's computer was an abuse of discretion and deprived defendant Brad Cooper of his state and federal constitutional due process right to present a defense.

Court's ruling: "We cannot find sufficient evidence in the record to support the trial court's exclusion of Ward's testimony, as indicated above, for any of the three prongs of the Howerton analysis. <u>The Google Map files recovered from Defendant's laptop were perhaps the most important pieces of evidence admitted in the trial. We hold that the trial court abused its discretion in excluding Ward from testifying, relying on the State's own evidence, to his opinion that the Google Map files recovered from Defendant's laptop had been tampered with.</u> Assuming arguendo the trial court did not abuse its discretion in disallowing Ward from giving his opinion concerning the Google map files, we hold that <u>the trial court erred in violation of the constitution of the United States and North Carolina</u>."

III. Denial of the defense motion for pretrial discovery of the files of the state's computer examiners and motion at trial production of the data created by the state's computer examiners in September 2008 and first disclosed to the defense during trial on April 13, 2011, was error which deprived defendant Brad Cooper of his state and federal constitutional right to confrontation and his due process right to present a defense.

Court's ruling: "The trial court could have conducted an in camera review of the requested discovery, and sealed the portions withheld to include in the record on appeal for the Court to review. Even in the face of a compelling State interest in keeping records confidential, due process might compel discovery, depending on how material the records are to a defendant's defense."

"We hold that on these facts due process required that the trial court at least examine the records in camera to determine whether that should be provided to the defense." We do not question that NCGS 15A-908 may serve to prevent discovery of certain otherwise discoverable material, based upon the concerns in the present case. In this case, however, we find the blanket exclusion ordered by the trial court unsupported by the record we have before us. "Regarding Judge Gessner's use of national security to prohibit the defense from viewing the state expert's duplication of the Google map search, it was error for the trial court to shut down this line of questioning without ascertaining how, or if, national security or some other legitimate interest outweighed the probative value of this information to Defendant. On remand, the trial court must determine with a reasonable degree of specificity how national security or some other legitimate interest would be compromised by discovery of particular data or materials, and memorialize its ruling in some form allowing for informed appellate review."[138]

On September 3, 2013, the North Carolina Court of Appeals ruled unanimously and strongly in Brad's favor on all three counts and ordered a new trial. Understand that it is difficult to win an appeal. The judge was so completely out of line that three seasoned judges on the North Carolina Court of Appeals were convinced that Brad's constitutional rights had been so severely violated that the verdict could not be trusted. They believed that had the jury heard from the defense experts, the verdict could have been different. This was a big win for Brad Cooper. The State chose to delay things further by filing a petition for discretionary review to the North Carolina Supreme Court but it was denied in January, 2014 so Brad was entitled to a new trial.

Though the appeal was won on the three described issues, here is the complete list of items considered by Brad's appeal attorney, Ann Peterson. It is included to highlight the severity of the judge's biased rulings throughout the case.

1. Denial of the motion to compel discovery of the education, training and experience of the examiner that examined the Blackberry and SIM card.
2. Denial of discovery request and motions to compel made and heard on March 22-23, 2010, August 27, 2010, and February 4, 2011.
3. Refusal to seal for appellate review discovery information the court has denied defense.
4. Refusal to examine in camera discovery information the court has denied the defense.

5. Refusal to disclose the existence of police interviews with Mr. Cooper's child, who made statements to a third party that were exculpatory.

6. Refusal to order disclosure of full and specific information in the hands of law enforcement and prosecutors concerning a person who might have had ill will toward Ms. Cooper stemming from a sexual relationship or desired sexual relationship with her.

7. Refusal to order disclosure of relevant information held by a family law litigator hired by defendant's in-laws.

8. Refusal to order disclosure of the training and experience of a police investigator who claims he accidentally erased the contents of Ms. Cooper's cell phone.

9. Refusal to order disclosure of information obtained by the police from Mr. Cooper's employer, Cisco Systems.

10. Refusal to order disclosure of the protocols and methods utilized by prosecution computer experts.

11. Refusal to order full disclosure of the "complete files of all law enforcement and prosecutorial agencies involved in the investigation of the crimes committed or the prosecution of the defendant" as required by G.S. 15A-901(a)(1)

12. Granting the motion to quash the subpoenas of the FBI agents.

13. Excused juror Jones

14. Not restoring a preemptory when a regular juror was excused prior to all the alternates being selected.

15. Denial of the defendant's motion in limine on Mrs. Cooper's statements to various witnesses.

16. Allowing various witnesses to testify to statements made to them by Nancy Cooper.

17. Denial of the right to cross-examine Ms. Duncan about Bella saying she saw her Mom that morning.

18. Denial of the right to cross-examine Ms. Duncan about Nancy Cooper's statement after John Pearson spent the night, "Where are my pants?"

19. Denial of the right to cross-examine Ms. Adam about whether Nancy sent her emails and whether Nancy stood people up.

20. Allowing Officer Dismukes to testify that defendant exercised his right to an attorney when asked to consent to search.

21. Denial of the defendant's right to cross-examine Officer Dismukes about Defendant's exhibits 10-20.

22. Not allowing the defendant to introduce or cross-examine Officer Dismukes about statements made by Bella about seeing her mother that morning.

23. Not allowing the defendant to cross-examine Officer Dismukes about Mr. Pearson changing his story when questioned.

24. Denial of a continuance.

25. Allowing Mr. Patterson to testify as an expert without providing a report.

26. The trial court's constant and continual comments about what a witness has testified to or what the evidence shows or why certain evidence is relevant, admissible or not.

27. Allowing the introduction of the computers and other electronic items into evidence with no assurances that the data contained on them is what was contained on them when seized.

28. Restricting the cross-examination of Detective Young.

29. Allowing the State to introduce a portion of the deposition of defendant without proper redaction.

30. Not allowing the defendant to cross-examine Detective Young about receiving a letter from Mr. Kurtz' partner about preserving data on the Blackberry.

31. Allowing introduction of testimony by Detective Young on the defendant's exercise of his right to silence and his right to an attorney.

32. Allowing Detective Young to testify to what Dr. Brannon (Nancy's OB/GYN) told him.

33. Not allowing the defendant to cross-examine Detective Young about the fact that questions were faxed to the defendant and the defendant answered the questions.

34. Allowing the State to question Ms. Fetterolf about pictures that defendant's counsel allegedly put on the web site.

35. Allowing Mr. Fetterolf to testify that Mr. Kurtz gave the cell phone to Ms. Cooper at a hearing.

36. Allowing Ms. Lister to testify that Nancy was stressed out about having kids.

37. Allowing Dr. Hackeling to testify to putting on a sports bra to show the jury.

38. Allowing Mr. Giralt to testify about an email on defendant's computer for allegedly buying an FXO.

39. Allowing Agent Johnson's testimony about tests on computers which were not provided in discovery.

40. Denial of a motion to continue in order to cross-examine Agent Johnson.

41. Denial of a Motion to strike Agent Johnson's and Agent Chappell's testimony.

42. Denial of the defendant's request for underlying data for tests performed by Agent Johnson and Chappell.

43. Allowing the State to introduce evidence of a bookmark "A practical guide to suicide."
44. Allowing the State to introduce the fact that defendant did not consent to a search and that he exercised his right to remain silent.
45. Allowing State's Exhibits 632 and 633 into evidence.
46. Not allowing the defendant to make his full offer of proof.
47. Allowing Detective Daniels to testify about information he received about a "nanner" account.
48. Not allowing defendant to cross-examine Detective Daniels about Defendant's Exhibit 53.
49. Denial of the defendant's right to cross-examine Detective Daniels about Defendant's Exhibit 97.
50. Allowing the State to proceed on a motion in limine to qualify Mr. Ward outside the presence of the jury.
51. Prohibiting the defendant's expert, Mr. Ward, from testifying as a forensic expert to interpret the FBI data.
52. Not allowing the defendant to have Agent Johnson perform an experiment in court.
53. Not allowing Mr. Ward to testify about whether Mr. Cooper's computer had been altered or tampered with.
54. Using National Security as a means of prohibiting the defendant from obtaining necessary discovery and his ability to defend himself.
55. Denial of the defendant's motion for mistrial.
56. Denial of the defendant's motion to recuse the trial judge.
57. Not allowing Mr. Ward to testify about the data he can or has reviewed, FBI data.
58. Allowing Mr. Ward to be cross-examined with his Facebook page.

59. Not allowing the defendant to call Mr. Masucci as a witness and/or expert, and denying the defendant to present his defense.
60. Allowing Mr. Miglucci to testify in rebuttal.
61. Denial of the motions to dismiss for failure to prove all the element of the offense of first degree murder.
62. Allowing the prosecutor to make improper comments during closing arguments.

{ 25 }

The Final Legal Proceedings and Author's Thoughts

In January 2014, after the Supreme Court upheld the Court of Appeals decision, Brad was transferred from prison to the Wake County Jail. That is the typical procedure for defendants awaiting trial. Unfortunately, since he is a Canadian citizen and his green card had expired, he was forced to be held without bond due to ICE requirements. It's much easier for a person to work on their defense case from outside the prison, but Brad was not allowed that option.

Conditions in jail naturally are poor but especially from a communication standpoint. One can't visit directly with family and friends. All visits are through a video feed, so even if Brad's parents visited from Canada, he would not be able to sit down and talk to them face to face. There was no possibility of any discreet conversations. All phone calls are recorded, so he could not freely discuss any concerns he may have had about facing a new trial.

Shortly after the Supreme Court decision, attorney James Freeman was appointed to represent Brad. Freeman does not appear to have a strong background in criminal law. His specializations are listed as personal injury, civil, business and employment law. It is unclear why an attorney from the capital public defender's list was not assigned to Brad's case, as one would have expected.

The State was working on a plea deal and shockingly, a court date for the acceptance of the deal was set before Brad was even presented with the offer. What was going on? Equally as outrageous, the media also reported that Brad was considering a deal before he received the offer. He actually learned about the offer from the news. Brad's parents learned about the offer from this author. The system was letting Brad down once again.

At that point, though Freeman had been representing Brad for nine months, he had not even finished reading the trial transcript; he had not reviewed the discovery, and he had only visited Brad four times. Further, he did not file a single motion on Brad's behalf. He should have filed a motion for the FBI discovery materials that the Court of Appeals declared Brad was entitled to. He should have filed for a change of venue. He should have filed several motions in anticipation of trial, but he did not.

To make matters worse, Brad learned that he would be facing the same judge in the new trial. Consider the enormity of that. This judge was completely slammed by the Court of Appeals. His bias was so severe and so obvious. What does Wake County do? They appoint the same judge for the new trial! It appeared to be a set-up, a continuation of the railroading and more evidence to suggest that Brad Cooper had in fact been framed. Imagine having to endure another trial with the same judge who demonstrated so much bias and ignorance about the "technical stuff" throughout the first trial. Again, Freeman could have filed a motion for Judge Gessner to recuse himself, but he didn't bother to do that either. How could Brad possibly have any hope of receiving a fair trial? How could he face the same dishonest people again?

The Offer

In exchange for agreeing to plead guilty to second degree murder, Brad would be freed in seven years. Another year would be removed if he agreed to allow Nancy's sister and her husband to adopt his daughters, knocking it down to six years. He was facing six years versus *life*. He could take his chances with a new trial and fight to prove his innocence, but he knew that if he lost again, he would have to go through the lengthy appeal process all over again with no guarantees. He was rightfully nervous in light of everything that happened to him the first time around.

Consider the decision he was facing. On an even playing field, it would be a no-brainer certainly to go to trial again, but we don't have an even playing field. Consider everything he faced the first time around – a dishonest investigation filled with fabrications, tunnel vision, destroyed evidence, witness coercion, witness alliances, a biased judge and prosecutors who did everything possible to block the defense case. Would anyone feel comfortable heading back to a courtroom with the same players? It is a frightening thought.

Brad could have requested a new attorney, but that would delay things at least another year while he/she got up to speed with the case. The prosecutors told the court that they were not ready to go to trial, so likely it would have been at least a year or two away, thus leaving Brad only four more years to guaranteed freedom – four more years until he could be free to go back to Canada to his family and leave this nightmare behind. Brad did not believe that he could ever receive a fair trial, so in September 2014, he accepted the plea deal. He agreed to relinquish his parental rights, sadly, because he knew there was very little likelihood that he would ever be able to get his children back. By the time he gets out, they will be old enough to make their own decisions on whether or not to see him.

I believe Brad made the only sensible decision *in a very unfair judicial system*. There is no telling what tactics prosecutors may have pulled in a second trial. There are many cases where prosecutors make deals with jailhouse snitches. They offer them lighter sentences in exchange for false testimony to aid their conviction. My personal belief is that the State was never going to allow the truth to come out – proof that the FBI had evidence that the map search was not authentic. They were not going to allow the Cary Police Department's reputation to be further tarnished. They probably would have found a way to railroad Brad again, and it would have been easy with the same judge. It is not supposed to be this way.

It is important to point out that there is no recourse for official misconduct. If one wins an appeal, they may be granted a new trial, but the same players are still involved. Everyone that had a role in the wrongful conviction is still there, waiting to do it all over again – the same police officers, the same prosecutors and in Brad's case, the same judge, only this time they're angry for being slammed by the Court of Appeals. The appeals process does not address police, prosecutorial or judicial misconduct. In fact, nothing addresses it.

Part of the reason that prosecutors get by with misconduct is because they have immunity. Judge Alex Kozinski referenced a case from 1983 that gave prosecutors immunity from misconduct.

> In Imbler v. Pachtman, a divided Supreme Court held that prosecutors are absolutely immune from damages and liability for misconduct they commit when performing the traditional activities of a prosecutor. Under Imbler, prosecutors cannot be held liable, no matter how badly they misbehave, for actions such as withholding exculpatory evidence, introducing fabricated evidence, knowingly presenting perjured testimony and bringing charges for which there is no credible evidence. All are immune from liability[139]

For the time being, prosecutors continue to get away with unlawful prosecutions because there is no one to prosecute *them*. I had no idea this was occurring until I watched this trial. Now that I know about it, I feel driven to help the wrongfully convicted tell their stories. After the Cooper trial, many people felt as outraged as I did. Some contacted the Attorney General to complain about the injustice. Of course, he did nothing about it. I personally contacted the Cary mayor, the town manager, the FBI and the Attorney General. The only response I received was from the mayor who stated that I didn't hear all the testimony. Since then I have read the entire trial transcript, and it has not changed my opinion that there was rampant misconduct in this case.

During Brad's plea hearing, ADA Cummings admonished Brad for "wasting so many taxpayer dollars" on this case, stating that he should have just accepted the plea deal when it was offered before the first trial. The unbelievable arrogance! He was basically saying, "How dare you fight for your innocence!" After that, I filed FOIA (Freedom of Information Act) requests to all of the agencies I could think of. I sent one to Cary Police, to the SBI and the District Attorney's office. According to FOIA policies, citizens are entitled to see the expenses incurred by government officials. The only agency that did not respond was the DA Office, even though they were legally required to provide the requested information.

I believe Brad Cooper is innocent based on everything I have so carefully researched these past four years. I have never found one thing that made me question my belief. I have researched several other wrongful conviction cases, and it's becoming easy to spot the pattern. When you start seeing signs of a dishonest investigation – lying, prosecutors misstating evidence and tunnel vision, it almost without fail means the person is innocent, and in many cases there is physical evidence that ultimately proves the defendant's innocence. *Unethical* prosecutors use these tactics because they have a win-at-all-cost-mentality, and when there isn't evidence of guilt, they make it up. The mentality exists because the District Attorney is a political position and voters demand a "tough on crime" stance, so they pressure their prosecuting attorneys to win and reward them with promotions. Losing a case like this would have been a disaster for the DA's office, but they should have never tried the case in the first place.

My hope is that people will learn from this and not be so willing to trust the system and that people will realize that what happened to Brad could happen to anyone. I hope that Brad's daughters will one day learn the truth. Brad loves them and would have never hurt their mother. The entire thing was a devastating travesty of justice.

Unfortunately, once someone is convicted of a crime, there will always be people who will believe the person is guilty, even if they are completely exonerated. There's something psychological about it, or maybe it's an innate trust in the government, that the justice system wouldn't purposely try an innocent person. For those who still attempt to claim Brad is guilty by trying to justify reasons for the many anomalies found on his computer, there is no way to ever trust anything found on that machine. There would be no debate or discussion had investigators done an honest job. No one can deny that Brad's rights were severely violated and that the State of North Carolina squandered any hope of his being able to prove that he was framed when they delayed the sharing of the hard drive. There will continue to be efforts to analyze the hard drive to learn as much as possible about how the files may have been planted on the machine, but there is already an overwhelming amount of irrefutable tampering evidence. This case permanently affected my life because it opened my eyes to the state of our justice system. I now plan to do everything I can to expose the injustices and to help those wrongfully convicted of crimes, because I can't think of many things worse than an innocent person in prison at the hands of corrupt government officials.

Cooper Family October 2006

Carol Cooper, Brad, Katie and Bella, 2008

Terry Cooper with Katie, Fall 2006

Brad, aged 10, with his mother, Carol Cooper

Coopers' house in Cary

Brad, Nancy, Bella and Katie

Brad, Nancy, Bella and Katie

Terry, Carol, Bella, Nancy, Katie, and Brad Fall 2007

ABOUT THE AUTHOR

Lynne recently published her second true crime novel, *Absence of Evidence* — An Examination of the Michelle Young Murder Case. She resides in Raleigh, North Carolina, with her husband and two sons. She graduated from Kent State University with a Bachelor of Science degree in Chemistry.

Lynne became concerned about the state of the U.S. justice system after following some local trials and began researching cases and advocating for the wrongfully convicted. She is currently doing paralegal work with The Deskovic Foundation for Justice, an organization that seeks to exonerate innocent defendants.

If you enjoyed the book, Lynne would very much appreciate a review at any retailer's website that carries the books.

Contact: lablanchard@nc.rr.com

Blogs: justiceforbradcooper.wordpress.com

stopwrongfulconvictions.wordpress.com

Website: justiceforbradcooper.com

YouTube Channel: Wrongful Convictions

Published in September, 2016

Michelle Young was living the American dream. The former NC State cheerleader was married to Jason. They had a beautiful two year old daughter and a son on the way. The couple enjoyed a comfortable life in the quiet Enchanted Oaks community of Raleigh, North Carolina.

It was autumn—a time for football games and holiday plans, but on November 3, 2006 Michelle was found beaten to death in her home. It shook the community and quickly attracted national attention.

Police immediately began investigating Jason . . . but he was out of town at the time of the murder. Would they discover enough evidence to solve the crime? Discover the facts about this fascinating and controversial case.

Endnotes

[1] http://wrongfulconvictionsblog.org/2012/12/05/the-dangers-of-tunnel-vision/

[2] Bates stamps 03129, 11350, 00324, 12022, 11632, 10956

[3] Bates stamp 00324

[4] Bates stamp 12022

[5] http://www.nbcphiladelphia.com/news/local/FRI-Pennypack-Mother-Joggers-Death-270444101.html

[6] http://www.nbcnews.com/id/25723445/ns/msnbc_tv-msnbc_tv_commentary/t/who-killed-nancy-cooper/#.VZAATUaQm1x

[7] http://www.nbcnews.com/id/25723445/ns/msnbc_tv-msnbc_tv_commentary/t/who-killed-nancy-cooper/#.VZAATUaQm1x

[8] Bate stamps 000126, 11014, 11714

[9] Bate stamp 11603

[10] Bate stamp 11020

[11] Bates stamp 00771

[12] Diana Duncan deposition

[13] http://www.wral.com/asset/news/local/2008/09/29/3638836/1222727302-NancyCooperAutopsyReport.pdf

[14] http://standdown.typepad.com/weblog/2010/08/misoncduct-at-the-north-carolina-sbi-forensic-lab.html

[15] Bates stamp 10944

[16] Bates stamp 11620

[17] Bates stamp 11620

[18] Bates stamp 648

[19] Jessica's deposition

[20] Bates stamp 643

[21] https://www.ohiobar.org/ForPublic/Resources/LawYouCanUse/Pages/LawYouCanUse-90.aspx

[22] Bates stamp 8663

[23] Bates stamp 03935

[24] Bates stamp 11336

[25] Bates stamp 11388

[26] Bates stamp 00663

[27] Bates stamp 8882

[28] Brad's rebuttal affidavit 7/24/08

[29] Bates stamp 649

[30] Bates stamp 1352

[31] Bates stamp 11388

[32] Bates stamp 11522

[33] Bates stamp 14575

[34] Bates stamp 14567

[35] Bates stamp 647

[36] Bates stamp 8689

[37] Bates stamp 644

[38] Bates stamp 8689

[39] http://www.wral.com/asset/news/local/2008/07/17/3222032/1216322668-20080717151650387.pdf

[40] http://dig.abclocal.go.com/wtvd/cooper_affidavit.pdf

[41] http://dig.abclocal.go.com/wtvd/20080930155921.pdf

[42] Bates stamp 00645

[43] Bates stamp 649

[44] Trial transcript

[45] https://www.legalzoom.com/articles/the-basics-of-attorney-client-privilege

[46] https://en.wikipedia.org/wiki/Chain_of_custody

[47] CISSP Manual

[48] http://www.makeuseof.com/tag/what-is-wep-wi-fi-encryption-and-why-is-it-really-insecure-makeuseof-explains/

[49] http://www.webopedia.com/TERM/H/hashing.html

[50] roselawtx.wordpress.com

[51] http://www.wtae.com/blob/view/-/23868288/data/1/-/pt0s91/-/Robert-Ferrante-affidavit-details.pdf

[52] http://news.softpedia.com/news/Murderer-Arrested-With-Google-s-Help-49940.shtml

[53] https://justiceforbradcooper.wordpress.com/2012/01/13/computer-evidence-must-be-verified-to-stand-up-in-court/

[54] http://www.intaforensics.com/blog/2009/01/digital-forensics-helps-secure-murder-conviction/

[55]

http://www.wral.com/asset/news/news_briefs/2008/10/09/3706693/26782-Affidavit_of_Det._George_G._Daniels.pdf

[56] Bates stamp 11146

[57] Bates stamp 00646

[58] Bates stamp 8776

[59] Bates stamp 280

[60] Bates stamp 11484

[61] Bates stamp 12250

[62] Bates stamp 8669

[63] Amy Fitzhugh witness interview

[64] Bates stamp 8581

[65] Bates stamp 8617

[66] Bates stamp 652

[67] Bates stamp 9132

[68] Bates stamp 9130

[69] Bates stamp 11692

[70] Bates stamp 11702

[71] Bates stamp 11028
[72] Bates stamp 1368
[73] Bates stamp 8607
[74] Bates stamp 8621
[75] Bates stamp 10966
[76] Bates stamp 644
[77] Bates stamp 00663
[78] Bates stamp 10968
[79] Bates stamp 11670
[80] Bates stamp 8685
[81] Bates stamp 10922
[82] Bates stamp 15868
[83] Bates stamp 11638
[84] Bates stamp 11672
[85] Bates stamp 11672
[86] https://en.wikipedia.org/wiki/Alienation_of_affections
[87] Bates stamp 8842
[88] Bates stamp 11468
[89] Bates stamp 11470
[90] Bates stamp 8926
[91] Cooper motion for writ of certiorari
[92] Bates stamp 12250
[93] Bates stamp 12212
[94] https://justiceforbradcooper.files.wordpress.com/2015/09/red-flags-of-911-calls.pdf
[95] Bates stamp 294
[96] Bates stamp 8669
[97] Bates stamp 661
[98] http://www.ncbar.com/rules/rules.asp
[99] Bates stamp 11684
[100] Bates stamp 11216
[101] Bates stamp 15305
[102] C#088
[103] Bates stamp 15305
[104] Bates stamp 15305
[105] Bates stamp 11072
[106] https://justiceforbradcooper.files.wordpress.com/2015/09/0714_0001.pdf
[107] Bates stamp 12895
[108] Bates stamp 13251
[109] Brad Cooper interview with author
[110] Transcript page 4597

[111] Bates stamp 00142

[112] Bates stamp 00310

[113] https://justiceforbradcooper.files.wordpress.com/2011/11/blackberry_report1.pdf

[114] http://00d546c.netsolhost.com/ncpba/cary/

[115] Bates stamp 00570

[116] https://en.wikipedia.org/wiki/Spoliation_of_evidence

[117] Jay Ward's report

[118] Computer Crime, Investigation and the Law, page 64

[119] Jay Ward's Report Bates stamp 367

[120] Agent Chappell's report on tampering

[121] Trial transcript page 7093

[122] https://justiceforbradcooper.files.wordpress.com/2012/07/cursor-files.gif

[123] http://forensicswiki.org/wiki/Timestomp

[124] Jay Ward's report

[125] http://www.informationweek.com/ex-computer-consultant-convicted-in-google-murder-trial/d/d-id/1038396

[126] bates stamp 15558, Cary police powerpoint

[127] http://www.wral.com/news/local/story/2541602/#fAR78iAhvYAQxVsf.99

[128] https://www.law.cornell.edu/wex/brady_rule

[129] https://justiceforbradcooper.files.wordpress.com/2013/04/durie-affidavit.pdf

[130] https://msdn.microsoft.com/en-us/library/windows/desktop/aa365230%28v=vs.85%29.aspx

[131] Bates stamp 13492

[132] http://www.theatlantic.com/politics/archive/2015/04/csi-is-a-lie/390897/

[133] No - Cooper_Motion_to_Dismiss_PDR.pdf

[134] No - Cooper_Motion_to_Dismiss_PDR.pdf

[135] No - Cooper_Motion_to_Dismiss_PDR.pdf

[136] Court exhibit #5

[137] http://www.wral.com/specialreports/nancycooper/story/9677512/#xzV8Wjg3Uqo5j89z.99

[138] NC Court of Appeals decision 9/3/13

[139] http://georgetownlawjournal.org/files/2015/06/Kozinski_Preface.pdf (pg. 37)

Made in the USA
Middletown, DE
28 September 2018